Discover

Sky

John Bailey

ACKNOWLEDGEMENTS

Inspiration for the completion of *Discovering Skye* has not only come from the beautiful, awe-inspiring landscape but also from the numerous islanders that I have met. Many have provided me with a great awareness of the beauty and diversity of this magical island, a place where traditional values are still a part of everyday life.

I would like to thank each and every one that has taken time to talk about the island's past and present. I would especially like to acknowledge the following for their contribution and help in what has been a thoroughly rewarding experience. The peat-cutting process was admirably explained by Mr Jackson from Dunvegan, who took time out to demonstrate the craft of the peat cutter. My grateful thanks go to Gerry Akroyd MBE and the Skye Mountain Rescue Team for the detailed information and photographs supplied by Alan Law. The Skye Museum of Island Life Kilmuir, for the comprehensive detailed text on the museum, its history and for allowing the photographs to be used. A particular acknowledgement must go to Hugh MacLeod of MacLeod, 30th Clan Chief of Dunvegan Castle for not only the detailed text to ensure accuracy with reference to Dunvegan Castle but also for supplying the castle photography, in addition perhaps most significantly for taking time out to write the foreword. A note of thanks must also go to the boatmen at Dunvegan Castle for the highly informative trip around the loch to visit the seal colonies; their knowledge is second to none and provides a unique opportunity for stunning photography.

As with my previous publications special recognition has to go to Tina, who has spent immeasurable hours travelling with me around the island, striving to capture the perfect shot, and has contributed to a good deal of the photographs for *Discovering Skye*. To Nick, again for his contributions and helping with the equipment on some of the longer trails. Last but not least, I would like to again acknowledge Alex Morton and his colleagues at DB Publishing for their enthusiasm to publish *Discovering Skye*.

First published in Great Britain in 2011 by The Derby Books Publishing Company Limited, 3 The Parker Centre, Derby, DE21 4SZ.

ISBN 978-1-85983-847-1   Printed and bound by Melita Press, Malta.

Discovering Skye

John Bailey

Foreword by Hugh MacLeod of MacLeod

Photography by John and Tina Bailey

DB PUBLISHING

CONTENTS

Allt Coire Lagan begins its journey to Loch Brittle rising high under the shadow of Sgurr Dearg, at 3235ft one of 12 Munros on Skye. Sgurr Dearg, although one of the most challenging peaks on the Cuillin ridge, is within the capability of hillwalkers, except that is, the final 65ft which is the height of the narrow fin of rock known as the Inaccessible Pinnacle or In Pin, only accessible to climbers.

FOREWORD

The Isle of Skye attracts increasing numbers of visitors each year. The magnetic attraction of the island is derived from the majestic grandeur of its land and seascapes, its history and the rich cultural legacy of its people. Together they provide the perfect antidote for those in search of a respite from the pressures of the modern world.

Although much has changed since two of its earliest visitors, Dr Johnson and James Boswell, made their celebrated tour of the Hebrides in 1773, there is a timeless quality which pervades the island. As one old adage goes, 'Time on Skye is not the time you go by, but the time you remember.'

In his journal, Boswell remarked that they were 'sometimes relieved by a view of branches of the sea, that universal medium of connection amongst mankind' and the 'wild, moorish, hilly and craggy appearances which gave a rude magnificence to the scene.' That magnificent landscape which has inspired generations of writers, artists, climbers and walkers remains one of the few places in Europe where nature and not man is in control. It is a place where one can access a unique and solitary connection with the natural world.

John Bailey's informative and well-researched book, *Discovering Skye*, provides an insight into the magical places to explore and savour on the Isle of Skye.

Hugh MacLeod of MacLeod
Dunvegan Castle & Gardens
Isle of Skye

INTRODUCTION

In the 1920s and the 1930s H.V. Morton undertook a tour of Scotland driving a Bullnose Morris concluding on Skye where he believed Skye was 'The strangest place in the British Isles'. Looking for the perfect vista on which to end his journey, Morton wasn't disappointed rewarded with magnificent views from the lofty summits of the Cuillin.

H.V. Morton, author of *In Search of Scotland 1892–1979*

The Isle of Skye (Scottish Gaelic: *An t-Eilean Sgitheanach* or *Eilean a' Cheò*) is the largest and most northerly of the Inner Hebrides a group of islands bordering the north-west coast of Scotland. It is an island of immense contrasts, ranging from the magnificent rugged coast with cliffs that rise 1,000ft from the sea, tranquil sea lochs with jagged shorelines that continue deep inland, vast rolling moor land and the extraordinary geological features of the Trotternish Ridge. The culmination of the diverse landscape is complete with the majestic Cuillin, rising over 3,000ft above sea level. It is the continually shifting light creating an extraordinary variety of dramatic moods complementing the beautiful landscape, together with the island's sometimes brutal history and way of life, that has drawn me back to discover and share this wonderful island called Skye, alas not in a Bullnose Morris.

Our journey of discovery begins in the south at the nearest point to the mainland, Kylerhea, where you can still come over the sea to Skye in the traditional way. Skye has remarkably differing regions, and these can be categorised as the southern peninsula of Sleat, sometimes referred to as the garden of Skye, Minginish that encompasses the Cuillin, Duirinish, Waternish and Trotternish all major promontories. A main road heads north from the bridge at Kyleakin to the island capital Portree, straddling the coast and moorland, eventually reaching Uig, a major port to the Western Isles.

The Strathaird peninsula is the first port of call, found west of Broadford where a single-track road continues under the shadow of Bla Bheinn to reach the shore at Elgol. The Cuillin, 12 Munros (peaks above 3,000ft), have been described as the most untamed and scenic mountain range in Britain; when viewed from the shore at Elgol no one would dispute that statement. It is a majestic mountain range that I have been told should always be referred to as just the Cuillin. The Cuillin are made up of the Black Cuillin (the main ridge and Bla Bheinn) and the Red Cuillin, the smaller rounded hills that are separated by Glen Sligachan.

To the north west are the regions of Duirinish and Minginish, impressive peninsulas of rolling moorland and rugged, sparsely inhabited coastline. Durinish is home to the distinctive flat-topped mountains of MacLeod's Tables. The area is steeped in history, where the Highland Clearances have had a major influence on the peoples and the landscape. The north west is home to Dunvegan Castle, the ancestral home of Clan MacLeod, and is the oldest continually inhabited castle in Britain, set on a rocky outcrop on Loch Dunvegan with the tranquil waters providing a safe haven for a colony of seals.

Skye's most northerly peninsula, Trotternish, is a geologist's delight with its vast inland cliff running for over 20 miles, bedecked with mysterious pinnacles and peaks, the peninsula culminating with the spectacular cliffs above Rubha Hunish, the northernmost point of Skye.

The scenery of Skye is extraordinary, and so is the island's history. We learn about Bonnie Prince Charlie and how, despite a huge bounty on his head, he was never betrayed by the Highlanders. The Highland Clearances and how the crofters were to eventually acquire security of tenure. I have included eight walks of varying degree that allows one to experience Skye first hand, with detailed routes and full OS mapping. Weather conditions always need to be considered before setting out. Care is needed for the higher areas of Trotternish and the Cuillin, as mists can descend even on the clearest of days, making navigation difficult.

It is the dramatic landscape Skye has to offer, the fascinating history and the constantly changing moods of the weather and light that will live long in your memory should you visit, and leaves one with a constant desire to return.

John Bailey

The bridge opened in 1995, taking the place of the ferry service that had begun over a century earlier connecting Kyleakin on Skye to the mainland at Kyle of Lochalsh. The lighthouse, built in 1857, stands on the small island of Eilean Ban, the bridge casting a shadow on the lighthouse, seemingly mirroring the distant hills.

Over the sea to Skye

Speed, bonnie boat, like a bird on the wing, Onward! the sailors cry; Carry the lad that's born to be King, Over the sea to Skye.

Loud the winds howl, loud the waves roar, Thunderclaps rend the air; Baffled our foes stand by the shore, Follow they will not dare.

Though the waves leap, soft shall ye sleep, Ocean's a royal bed: Rocked in the deep, Flora will keep, Watch by your weary head.

Many's the lad fought on that day, Well the Claymore could wield: When the night came silently lay, Dead in Culloden's field.

Burned are their homes, exile and death, Scatter the loyal men; Yet ere the sword cool in the sheath, Charlie will come again.

The Scottish folk song tells the story of the escape of Charles Edward Stewart, 'Bonnie Prince Charlie', from Uist to Skye after his defeat at Culloden in 1746. Charlie, now a fugitive, was tracked down to South Uist, where Flora MacDonald had agreed to help smuggle the Prince to Skye in a small boat, dressed as her maid Betty Burke. The song was first published by Boulton and MacLeod in 1884. Ms Annie MacLeod first heard the Gaelic air *Cuchag nan Craobh* being sung during a boat trip across Loch Coruisk by her rowers; she wrote down the music and Sir Harold Boulton later penned the lyrics.

There is uncertainty as to when the first crossing to Skye would have been established, but the shortest route is to be found here between the mainland, just under two miles north of Glenelg and Kylerhea on Skye. The Kyle Rhea is a mere 600yds wide at this point and would have been used by drovers taking their Highland cattle on the long journey from the Hebrides south to the Lowlands. It is said that some cattle would be swept away, only to make landfall on the shore at Glenelg.

The road to Glenelg began life as a military road and is still noted today as such on OS maps, constructed to reach the barracks at Bernera, now a ruin dating from the 18th century. The present road follows much of the old route. The crossing from the mainland to Kylerhea was the popular route to Skye until the Victorian period of railway building opened up the Highlands, with the line eventually reaching Kyle of Lochalsh in November 1897. A main ferry port was then established at Kyleakin and remained the gateway to Skye until the opening of the bridge in 1995.

The present car and passenger ferry at Kylerhea began in 1934 and continues operating between Easter and October. Today, the ferry service is run by The Isle of Skye Ferry Community Interest Company using the only turntable ferry of its type in Britain, providing a traditional and romantic journey across the sea to Skye.

The traditional and romantic. The ferry operates from Easter to October crossing the Kyle Rhea from the mainland close to Glenelg, a short distance of only 600yds.

The flora of Skye is perhaps no more evident than on the Sleat peninsula, often referred to as the garden of Skye.

Sleat is the most southern peninsula, often overlooked on the visitors' journey to the mountainous region of the Cuillin. During late summer, the wild beauty of the quiet roads and coastal fringes of Skye are adorned by swathes of the brightly coloured orange-red flowers of the Montbretia, their display enhanced dancing in the gentlest of breezes. Originating from South Africa, having a variety of eight species, Montbretia was named after the French botanist Coquebert de Montbret (1780–1801).

Montbretia thrives in any soil conditions but will colonise best in coastal locations. Although naturalised throughout Britain for gardeners, Montbretia is ideal for growing in herbaceous borders, with the flowers excellent for cutting. The plant is hardy enough to survive as far north as the Hebrides. Forming dense clumps, with new corms continually produced below ground, the plants soon take a firm foothold on their location.

A quintessential highland scene from Sleat across the Kyle Rhea to Glenelg on the mainland. You may just spot the ruins of Bernera Barracks, dating from the 18th century.

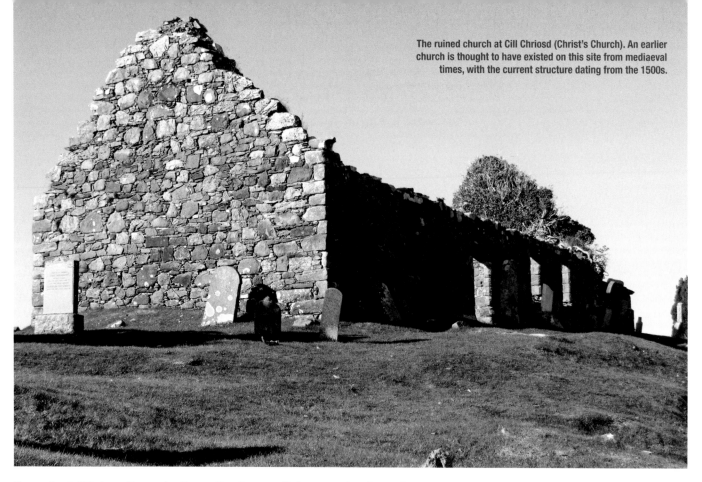

The ruined church at Cill Chriosd (Christ's Church). An earlier church is thought to have existed on this site from mediaeval times, with the current structure dating from the 1500s.

The small port of Elgol, as with many locations on Skye, has served in the past as the only route for supplies in and out of the area before the construction of the single track road from Broadford. The road twists and turns for over 14 miles, skirting the shore of Loch Slapin under the shadow of Blaven (Bla Bheinn), ahead of reaching the shore at Elgol, adding to the remote feel of the Strathaird peninsula. The Millennium stone that stands proud above Dunvegan was taken from the shores of Strathaird. The single-track road provides some notable views to contrast the coastal areas, meandering as it does along the valley of Strath Suardal to Loch Slapin, in particular at Loch Cill Chriosd. The ruined church at Cill Chriosd (Christ's Church) dates from the early 1500s, but it is believed an earlier structure stood on this site dating from mediaeval times. The church served as the parish church for Strathaird up until the mid-1800s.

A short distance from Cill Chriosd Church we find the shallow reed-filled waters of Loch Cill Chriosd beneath the slopes of Dearg Bheag, often reflected in its calm waters. Legend has it that these waters were home to an evil spirit that poisoned the waters, and anyone who washed in or drank the waters would succumb to harm. The waters became blessed from a visit by St Columba, and from that time on the waters were believed to be 'good for all'. Saint Columba, who had visited Skye during the 6th century, was also known as Colum Cille, meaning 'dove of the church'. A Gaelic Irish missionary monk, Saint Columba spread Christianity among the Picts during the Early Mediaeval Period. He is predominantly linked with the northern most part of Skye, although much better known for his association with the island of Iona.

The ancient stone work, some now clad with ivy, coupled with the almost manicured grass provides an undeniable sense of serenity.

13

Blaven

Beyond Loch Cill Chriosd the single-track road continues the length of the valley floor to reach Torrin, close to the shore of Loch Slapin, a picturesque sea loch under the shadow of Bla Bheinn. Pronounced Blah-yen and often referred to as Blaven, the mountain mass is an outlier of the main Cuillin ridge, providing a most striking backdrop to the loch when viewed from the southern shores. Blaven is one of 12 Munros on Skye, separated from the main Cuillin ridge by Glen Sligachan. The term Munro is synonymous with Scotland, named after the early leader of Scottish mountaineering Sir Hugh Munro, who set out to survey every peak above 3,000ft in 1891.

Sadly, Sir Hugh died before he could conquer all the peaks. Just two remained, one on Skye, the Inaccessible Pinnacle, and a lesser peak in the Cairngorms eventually downgraded in a survey carried out in 1981. The illustrious feat was secured by the Revd A.E. Robertson in 1901, 12 years after his first conquest. He did, though, complete them in what was described as an efficient manner, linking the peaks as opposed to a separate climb for each as Sir Hugh had undertaken. From a geologist's perspective, the Cuillin consists mainly of Gabbro and sheets of Dolerite, giving it a distinctive appearance. Gabbro is a hard rock, a delight for climbers as it provides good adhesion, but care is needed in the Cuillin as navigation by a compass can be unreliable.

Loch Cill Chriosd becomes a magical place with sunlight reflecting on the reeds and the shallow waters creating an illusion of diamonds in the loch.

The classic view of Bla Bheinn, across the blue waters of Loch Slapin. Bla Bheinn, also known as Blaven, is the most easterly peak of the Black Cuillin. Separated from the main Cuillin ridge by Glen Sligachan, Blaven is the highest of the surrounding mountains at 3,044ft, being one of 12 Munros on Skye.

After about 20 minutes' walking Loch Scavaig and Camas Fhionnairigh finally come into view, with the dwelling on the strand giving a true perspective to the scale of the scene. The awe-inspiring view encompasses the Cuillin ridge with the distant Gars-bheinn, Sgurrr na Stri and Camasunary.

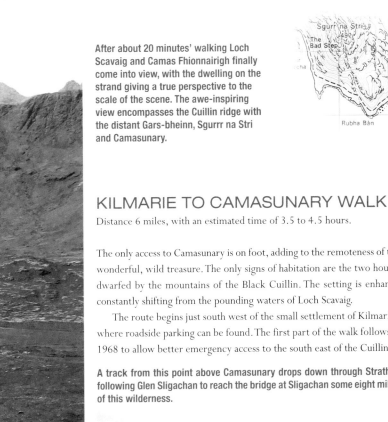

KILMARIE TO CAMASUNARY WALK

Distance 6 miles, with an estimated time of 3.5 to 4.5 hours.

The only access to Camasunary is on foot, adding to the remoteness of this wonderful, wild treasure. The only signs of habitation are the two houses standing on the strand of green sward, dwarfed by the mountains of the Black Cuillin. The setting is enhanced by the expanse of sand and pebbles, constantly shifting from the pounding waters of Loch Scavaig.

The route begins just south west of the small settlement of Kilmarie on the B8083 at grid reference 545 172, where roadside parking can be found. The first part of the walk follows the Land Rover track built by the army in 1968 to allow better emergency access to the south east of the Cuillin.

A track from this point above Camasunary drops down through Strath na Creitheach, and it continues under the shadow of Marsco following Glen Sligachan to reach the bridge at Sligachan some eight miles distant. My co-photographer helped to highlight the vastness of this wilderness.

17

Sgurr nan Gillean, the northern most peak of the Black Cuillin from Am Mam above Camasunary. The Gaelic meaning is said to be 'peak of the young men'. Completing the scene are Am Basteir and Bruach Frithe on the main ridge with Sgurr Hain in the foreground.

The track made it as far as Camasunary but has not been well maintained, helping to preserve the area's remoteness. It was proposed to continue the track around the coast to Loch Coruisk, destroying the Bad Step. The idea was met with a chorus of disapproval from mountaineers, who prevented further progress. The land is now owned by the John Muir Trust. Founded in 1983, the trust is dedicated to the protection of wild land for both nature and people. The trust also owns Kilmarie House, purchased from Ian Anderson, member of the 1970s rock band Jethro Tull, in 1994.

Cross the road to go through the gate where a plaque confirms the work of the army in 1968. The inviting track heads west–north west, with the early section a moderate steady rise following the contours of the land. Close to the shielings the track drops to ford a burn, then begins to gain height. Go through the gate to continue upward, passing a cairn. At this point the track becomes rougher and considerably steeper for the next mile. The rewards for the ascent are breathtaking views unfolding as you reach the pass of Am Mam. Ahead are the Cuillin, with the jagged peak of Sgurr nan Gillean in full view.

Bla Bheinn (Blaven). The south ridge provides the most scenic route to the summit. Abhainn nan Leac can be seen cascading downwards, flanked by Bla Bheinn and Slat Bheinn on a superb day in early summer.

The crystal-clear cool waters of Abhainn nan Leac rise high on the slopes of Bla Bheinn cascading just under 2 miles to Loch Scavaig. Seen here close to Camasunary, the journey is interrupted as the waters tumble over several rocky outcrops creating miniature waterfalls and numerous magical glistening pools on its journey to the sea. After heavy rains, the tranquil pools become impressive torrents.

The route to Camasunary is now clear to see. As you begin to descend, take the stony track down on your left – the route continuing ahead would lead you to Loch na Creitheach and eventually Glen Sligachan. The track now drops down taking a series of twists and turns to cross the river Abhainn nan Leac.

The first dwelling you see is privately owned, while at the far end of the beach is Camasunary bothy. Beyond the bothy, the Abhainn Camas Fhionnairigh flows into the sea. The river can be forded at low tide close to the remains of the old bridge should you wish to continue your journey into Loch Coruisk via the Bad Step. The bridge, part of the original plan to continue the track to Loch Coruisk, was soon destroyed by the forces of nature, with the Bad Step remaining intact.

What is certain is that you may well yearn to spend some considerable time here to take in the extraordinary tranquillity and feeling of seclusion of this beautiful setting.

Abhainn nan Leac looking west with the house at Camasunary dominated by the northern slope of Sgurr na Stri.

The waters of Abhainn nan Leac in a tranquil mood.

A true impression of peace and remoteness is achieved at Camas Fhionnairigh. Camasunary bothy dwarfed by Sgurr na Stri.

The Bothy Camasunary with the Cuillin as an inspirational backdrop. Left to right: Sgurr Hain, Marsco and Bla Bheinn.

The panorama from the shoreline out across Loch Scavaig takes in Rum some 12 miles distant and the much closer Isle of Soay, once a base for the author of *Ring of Bright Water*, Gavin Maxwell. The old Scandinavian name for Soay, *Sauda-ey* means 'Island of sheep'. Although a satellite of Skye, Soay is sometimes considered to be part of the Small Isles. The islanders were evacuated to Mull during 1953. Beyond lies the small island of Canna, the furthermost of the Small Isles from the mainland. During the summer months the strand is bedecked with cotton grass and bog myrtle, while sporadic clumps of fox glove can be seen striving to keep a foothold on the heather-clad hillside.

Cottongrass blowing in the gentle breeze on the strand at Camasunary helps to create a soothing atmosphere. Looking out south west across the glistening Loch Scavaig, you are rewarded with distant views to the Island of Rum. The shimmering sea reminds one of Gavin Maxwell's *Ring of Bright Water* with the much closer Island of Soay from where he once had a base.

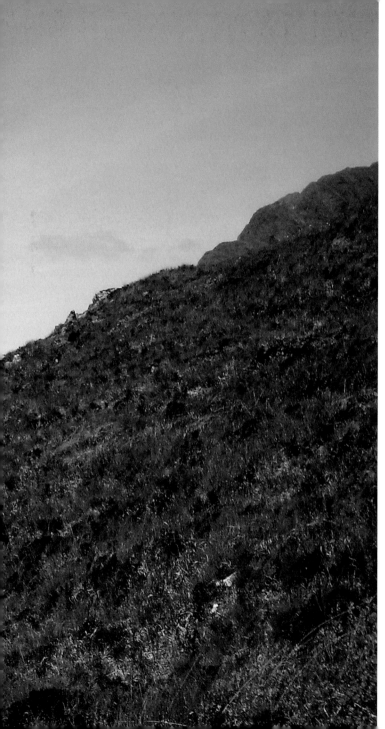

On the return part of the walk you will constantly find yourself pausing to glance back to the Cuillin.

The way back to the car park is taken by retracing your steps up the steep, twisting and turning track to the pass of Am Mam. You are, nevertheless, rewarded with equally spectacular views as the outward journey had provided. Once at Am Mam, the remainder of the route is an easy but pleasing descent following the Land Rover track back to the car park.

Our journey now continues southward along the single-track road with widespread views opening south east across to Loch Eishort and the Sleat peninsula, together with the distant mountains of the mainland beyond. After a distance of 3 miles, the road begins to descend in a series of twists and turns, to arrive on the coast at the scattered settlement and port of Elgol.

Views across loch Slapin to Sleat and the west coast of Scotland lie ahead on the concluding part of the walk.

The weather in sombre mood on the shore of Loch Scavaig at Elgol with the summit of Sgurr na Stri and Sgurr Hain highlighted during a brief sunny spell. The main ridge beyond and the summit of Marsco are obscured by cloud.

Camas Fhionnairigh. The two dwellings on the strand at Camasunary serve to highlight the vastness of the area when seen from Loch Scavaig, with Marsco dominating this view.

Elgol

The small crofting settlements of Elgol and Torrin were held by Clan MacKinnon, who fashioned a strong allegiance to the Jacobite uprising aimed at restoring James Stuart to the throne led by James VIII's son Prince Charles Edward Stuart, the 'Young Pretender' or 'Bonnie Prince Charlie'. Elgol is said to have been the last hiding place on Skye for the Prince before his escape to the mainland in 1746.

In 1745 Prince Charles Edward Stuart, aged 23, sailed to Scotland intent on raising an army of Highland Clans to restore the exiled Kings to the thrones of England, Scotland and Ireland. His forces were to take Perth, Edinburgh and Carlisle, but on reaching Derby without support promised from France and only limited cooperation from English Jacobites the Prince was forced to retreat back to Scotland. Outnumbered, the forces were defiant, eventually being heavily defeated when they met an army led by his cousin William Duke of Cumberland on Culloden Moor on 16 April 1746. By this time the Prince had a bounty on his head for £30,000, an enormous sum remembering this was over 250 years ago. Despite the bounty, the Prince was never betrayed by the Highlanders, who believed he would return to fight again.

After his escape from Uist to Skye, Bonnie Prince Charlie, still being pursued, eventually arrived at Elgol, having returned to Skye from Raasay. Captain John MacKinnon rowed the Prince across the Sound of Sleat to the mainland, aiding the Prince in his quest to seek safe refuge in France. Charles spent most of the remainder of his life in Italy, having been born in Rome.

Legend goes that the Prince gave MacKinnon a gift for his efforts, a recipe of his personal medicinal elixir. The recipe remained lost within the MacKinnon family for over a century until being produced locally as An Dram Buidheach, later to become the world famous liqueur, 'Drambuie'.

Like most of the Highlands, Elgol and Torrin were to later witness a dreadful exodus of the population during the infamous Highland Clearances.

Sgurr na Stri seen from the shore at Elgol across Loch Scavaig. A storm is about to set in, providing a fascinating light contrasting the shoreline the sea and the mountains.

Penning the right words to describe a view can at times be a quandary, as the trend can be to exaggerate the splendour of the occasion, but here from the shore at Elgol that could never be the case. The view out across Loch Scavaig north into the heart of the Cuillin cannot be equalled and can genuinely be described as sublime. Alfred Wainwright once stood on these shores and proclaimed that it was the best view in Britain, and very few if any would disagree with the great man's sentiments.

A visit to the heart of the Cuillin provides one with a pleasant conundrum: two options come to the fore, providing the visitor with equally impressive experiences that will live long in the mind. The more demanding of the two necessitates a start at Sligachan, walking the track that begins crossing the old packhorse bridge.

The awe-inspiring view across a breezy Loch Scavaig takes in the main Cuillin ridge, Sgurr na Stri the wide expanse of Camasunary, Sgurr Hain, Marsco and the lower slopes of Bla Bheinn. The fishing boat complements the scene.

A long-distance track runs through Glen Sligachan, following under the shadow of Marsco to then traverse the ridge of Druim Hain below the summit of Sgurr Hain. The route continues, descending from this point to reach the stepping stones crossing the Scavaig River to Loch Coruisk, a distance of over seven miles. Unless you are equipped to spend a night wild camping, you will need to be prepared to return to Sligachan by the same route, therefore planning of the walk is essential. Sufficient food and drink would need to be carried, as this is a truly remote wild place, and the route should only be attempted by experienced hill walkers, who can complete 15 miles of rough terrain in a single day.

The easier option, but nonetheless rewarding, is to take one of the boat trips from the jetty at Elgol, a captivating journey passing colonies of seals on the rocky shores of the tiny islets that adorn the loch. As you are drawn towards Loch Coruisk, the heather-clad mountains begin to take on their true appearance as giants rising abruptly from the sea.

Crossing the loch, it is easy to allow your mind to drift back to the 1870s, to the time when Annie MacLeod was taking a boat trip on the loch, and hear the beautifully haunting lyrics and music of *The Skye Boat Song*.

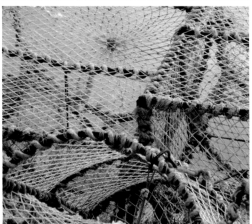

Lobster pots. The lobsters find their way in through a funnel to the main baited chamber; once in, they are unable to find their way back out. The lobster pots are dropped onto the sea bed with floating buoys to enable their later collection.

The classic view afforded from the shore at Elgol has to be one of the finest in Britain. The splendour of the Cuillin rise abruptly from the sea to their lofty heights above 3,000ft. Loch Coruisk lies at the foot of Druim nan Ramh, seen emanating from the main ridge in the centre of the Cuillin. The lone cloud in the distance is sitting directly above Am Bastier.

Gavin Maxwell established a shark fishing factory on Soay, having bought the island from the MacLeods of Dunvegan in 1945.

The rusting remains of the steam railway locomotive.

As we set out from Elgol to Loch Coruisk, the island offshore to the west is Soay, worth a detour into the small harbor on its north-west shore to view the remains of a long-abandoned shark fishing industry. In 1945 the author Gavin Maxwell establish a shark fishing factory on Soay, having bought the island from the MacLeods of Dunvegan. His attempt to turn it into a commercial venture would finally fail in 1948. The huge carcases would have been hauled ashore from the small harbour, with the livers used for oil, but the process required steam. A railway engine was brought by rail to Mallaig, finally reaching Soay by boat. The rusting steam railway locomotive can still be seen today, while the true story of Gavin Maxwell's adventures on Soay are told in his book *Harpoon at a Venture*.

The perfect way to get close to the numerous seals that inhabit Loch Scavaig is by kayak, seen here close to Eilean Reamhar.

Loch Coruisk

Loch Coruisk has been described as the most spectacularly sited loch in the British Isles, set in the basin of Coir Uisg. A closer look at Coire an Uaigneis and Sgurr a Mhadaidh on the main ridge make it clear to see why they are referred to as the Black Cuillin. During the ice age, immense glaciers would have gouged out the great corries, leaving behind the sheer ridges and peaks that make up the unique character of the Cuillin.

This inland loch provides the route deep into the eastern Cuillin and the Inaccessible Pinnacle, affectionately known as the Inn Pin. The track from Camasunary provides a shorter option when compared to the route from Sligachan, initially following the Land Rover track from Kilmarie on the Strathaird peninsula, a total distance of 5 miles, but presents a somewhat tough test, as it requires negotiating the Bad Step. The route from Camasunary skirts the western slopes of Sgurr na Stri, and here a slab of rock curves into the sea with no path around and requires some scrambling above deep open water.

A small jetty in Loch na Cuilce serves as a convenient stopping-off point for the boats from Elgol. Set close to the jetty is Loch Coruisk Memorial Hut, built in 1959 as a memorial for two young climbers who lost their lives while climbing on Ben Nevis. The hut is in the care of the Junior Mountaineering Club of Scotland, used as a base for excursions into the Cuillin, in particular Sgurr na Stri, Druim nan Ramh and Gars-bheinn.

Bright summer sun reflecting on the roof of Loch Coruisk Memorial Hut. The hut was built in 1959 as a memorial for two young climbers who lost their lives while climbing on Ben Nevis.

Loch Coruisk has been described as the most spectacularly sited loch in the British Isles set in the basin of Coir Uisg. During the ice age, immense glaciers gouged out the great corries leaving behind the sheer ridges and peaks.

The sheer slopes of Sgurr na Stri ascending abruptly from Loch nan Leachd give rise to the Bad Step, the most challenging part of the route from Camasunary to Loch Coruisk. In turn, they also provide a dramatic backdrop for the tiny islet of Sgeir Dorcha whose gentle oblique rocks provide the ideal setting for seals to laze at the water's edge.

Our journey continues away from the awe-inspiring scenery of Loch Scavaig, returning under the shadow of Blaven to the village of Broadford, where we rejoin the main road running from Kyleakin to Uig. As we know, Kyleakin was the main gateway to Skye before the opening of the bridge in 1995, with a ferry service from Kyle of Lochalsh. The main route to the port of Uig, a distance of some 50 miles, starts just west of Kyleakin, hugging the coast at the foot of the mountains between Broadford and Sligachan. Magnificent coastal scenery is afforded, with views across the Inner Sound to Scalpay and Raasay. The road was built in the 1820s by Thomas Telford as part of the government's plans for road and bridge building in the Highlands.

Impressive waterfalls cascade alongside the road as it climbs through the glen between Beinn Dearg Mhor and Druim nan Cleochd. As the last snows of winter melt from the mountains, the waterfalls provide a spectacular sight accompanied by a thunderous sound. One such encounter is above Loch Ainort as the road begins to climb steeply, negotiating a sharp bend. Many tributaries feed Allt Coire nam Bruadaran, beginning their journey high upon the slopes of Marsco, cascading just over 2 miles to Eas a' Bhradain before entering Loch Ainort.

As we approach Sligachan, the dominate shape of Glamaig, one of the Red Hills comes into full view, the road circumnavigating the eastern, northern and western slopes before entering Sligachan. Glamaig, at 2,543ft, was the site of a notable achievement in 1899 when Thapa a Ghurkha ran barefoot from Sligachan to the summit and back in 75 minutes. His feat was doubted by some, so completing the run again he somehow managed to achieve it in a remarkable time of 55 minutes. During July an annual race is now held, and Thapa's record stood proud until the 1980s.

As early winter snow melts from the mountains, waterfalls provide a spectacular sight, accompanied by a thunderous sound.

Sligachan

The scenery at Sligachan does not disappoint. It is a most pleasing setting, with the Cuillin providing a constant changing backdrop for the old pack horse bridge and one of the most popular routes into the Cuillin. The hotel at Sligachan was built as a coaching inn around 1830 and rapidly became a haven for early gentlemen climbers. The correct pronunciation for Sligachan, so I have been told, is 'Slig-a-han'. Glen Sligachan separates the loftier Black Cuillin from the more rounded Red Cuillin, with the exception of Blaven at 3,044ft, as we know one of 12 Munros on Skye, The distinction of the highest peak belongs to Sgurr Alasdair at 3,259ft, translated its meaning is the Peak of Alexander, named after Alexander Nicholson who made the first ascent in 1873. The ridge extends for over 6 miles, has 10,000ft of ascent and is graded as a 'very difficult rock climb'.

H.V. Morton said of the Cuillin, 'It seems as if nature when she hurled the Coolins up into the light of the sun said. I will make mountains which shall be the essence of all that can be terrible in mountains. I will pack into them all the fearful shapes. Their scarred ravines, on which nothing shall grow, shall lead up to towering spires of rock, sharp splinters shall strike the sky along their mighty summits, and they shall be formed of rock unlike any other rock so that they will never look the same for very long, now blue, now grey, now silver, sometimes seeming to retreat or to advance, but always drenched in mystery and terrors.'

Marsco, standing over 2,350ft, seen here sporting its winter coat, creating a most delightful backdrop for the old pack horse bridge. Sligachan became a haven for early gentlemen climbers with the advent of a coaching inn built around 1830.

The lofty peak of Sgurr nan Gillean 3,167ft is obscured by swirling mist, viewed from Loch nan Eilean.

A classic Cuillin view is afforded from Sligachan, where a track to Glenbrittle passes the remote Alltdearg House on route to Coir a Mhadaidh at the heart of the Cuillin. The peaks of Sgurr nan Gillaen, Am Bastier and Sgurr Bhastier dominant the skyline. Prevailing westerly winds and cloudy days on Skye will inevitably mean that the lofty Cuillin is obscured from view; however, surreal conditions occur when high-level cloud and swirling mists form above and below the summits. The dark summits seemingly appear from nowhere, only to fade away a few moments later, and the ridge with its many peaks takes on an eerie manifestation in contrast to clearer days that offer uninterrupted views of the entire ridge.

The Black Cuillin are the most spectacular and dangerous mountains in Britain. The higher peaks should only be attempted by experienced climbers, although the lower slopes will provide breathtaking mountain scenery without too much difficulty, providing you are fully prepared and equipped. Should you decide to venture to the loftier peaks and lack experience, then the prudent option would be to hire the services of a guide.

A track to Glenbrittle and Coir a Mhadaidh at the centre of the Cuillin passes Alltdearg House. The classic Cuillin view, although Squrr nan Gillean is covered in mist revealing Am Basteir and Sgurr a Bhasteir far right.

Skye Mountain Rescue Team

The visitor's book at the Sligachan Hotel records the first mountain rescue incident on Skye in 1870 when a man fell and died while descending Sgurr nan Gillean.

Between the years of 1870 and 1930 there were three further fatalities recorded in the visitor's book. The years from 1930 onward were to witness increasing numbers of visitors to the mountains and with this came increasing incidents and fatalities. During the war years there was little mountaineering activity, but with visitors to the mountains increasing again during the 1950s the first volunteer rescue team was established on Skye. Jonacks MacKenzie, the Portree postman, led a team of local shepherds, ghillies and policemen. By this time the first RAF Search and Rescue helicopters were operating alongside the volunteers. In the 1960s Pete Thomas took over as Team Leader, a role he held for over a decade, and subsequently John MacLeod in 1971 for an interim year. John Macleod later received an MBE from the Queen for services to mountain rescue after serving as Skye Mountain Rescue Team Chairman for many years. In 1972 the current Team Leader, Gerry Akroyd, took on this role and continues in this post today. In January 2010 Gerry was awarded an MBE for services to mountain rescue in the Queen's New Year's Honours list.

The 35-strong members of the Skye Mountain Rescue Team are local men and women from all over the island who give up their time to assist walkers and climbers in a time of emergency. The team members are all volunteers and receive no payment or retainer fee.

The team has two purpose-built huts, one in Glenbrittle and another at Sligachan, which were built with the generous help of the Order of St John; these act as base stations and control centres during rescues. The Skye Mountain Rescue Team is a registered charity, and their work is supported financially by a mixture of public

Practising stretcher work in Cuillin.

The new Coastguard helicopter.

donations, some grant aid from the Mountain Rescue Committee of Scotland toward training costs, support from other charities and fundraising to equip and run their team.

When someone is in trouble on the hills the police are called, and if it requires a mountain rescue callout Skye Mountain Rescue Team are alerted by telephone to meet at a specific point.

Team members receive regular training in skills such as first aid, navigation, rope-work, working with helicopters, and winter mountaineering. Members of the team provide a wealth of diverse skills, including a search and rescue dog handler (SARDA), a team doctor, rope access specialists and several mountain leaders and guides.

Mountain safety is paramount, and the Cuillin should not be underestimated. Always be prepared to turn back should mists begin to descend. Adequate clothing is essential and a good pair of mountain boots. Plenty of food and two litres of fluids should be carried to cover the unexpected. Before attempting to set out, ensure you are familiar with a good map and how to use it. A compass should be carried, but magnetic properties along the Cuillin ridge and in the corries can render them unreliable. You should always ensure someone knows your intended route and expected time of return.

The Skye team carries and maintains a great deal of rescue equipment. Much of this equipment has to be replaced on a regular basis e.g. ropes, helmets, oxygen and Entinox cylinders for pain relief, first aid equipment and batteries. More expensive items like stretchers, casualty bags and radios also need renewal when damaged or outdated. To meet these recurring expenses their annual running costs are in the region of £25,000 per year.

The Skye Mountain Rescue Team has two main bases located at Sligachan and Glenbrittle, which were built with the generous help of the Order of St John. These act as base stations and incident control centres during rescues.

The old farm buildings at the head of Gleann Oraid now showing signs of weathering, their dark red painted finish giving way to blue-grey and rusting hues now merging into the landscape, creating a striking foreground to the Cuillin.

As we continue north west from Sligachan, extended views of the Cuillin ridge open up from Glen Drynoch. Our next destination, Minginish, is home to Glenbrittle and Talisker Bay, both only accessible along single-track roads from the B8009 at Carbost. As we know, Glenbrittle is home to one of the two mountain rescue posts on Skye and for good reason; Glenbrittle is perhaps the most popular route for several excursions into the Cuillin. Hill walkers can, with care, access many of the lower slopes to marvel at the spectacular mountain scenery, without the need for scrambling, while experienced rock climbers continue to the loftier peaks.

The Cuillin in different guises. The variety of the rugged Cuillin scenery encompasses craggy peaks and picturesque waterfalls, while a huge variety of delicate flora emerges from the seemly unforgiving landscape. One such plant is Devils-bit Scabious, so called because the Devil was said to have bitten off the rootstock out of spite for the roots herbal powers.

Preshal More stands more than 1,000ft overlooking Gleann Oraid and Talisker.

TALISKER BAY WALK

Distance 6 miles, with an estimated time of 3–3.5 hours

Leaving behind the mountainous region of central Skye, we now discover an entirely different but equally magnificent landscape, one akin to what would be most people's perception of a remote island off the north-west coast of Scotland, a landscape of rolling moorland, rugged sea cliffs, prominent hills and beautiful glens. Preshal More stands more than 1,000ft overlooking Talisker and Gleann Oraid and is the dominant feature on this amble following the glen down to the sea, with the River Talisker close at hand. The walk begins by roadside parking at the top of Gleann Oraid at grid reference 353 304, taking care not to park in a passing place.

The route is a there-and-back walk and, if taken during spring through to summer, the moorland and cliffs are alive with an eye-catching display of wild flowers that at times reproduce a Dorset meadow. Vast swathes of wild hyacinths create a carpet of pale blue, while cottongrass with their hair like seed heads provide a continual display of dancing drifts of white, even in the slightest of breeze. As with most of Skye, the coastal fringes are awash with thrift, creating irregular patterns of deep to pale pink, with the often azure sea as a stunning backdrop. An overabundance of other wild flowers, some unique to the Hebrides, can be seen growing in the most unusual of places, looking at their best set against the lush green moorland or contrasting deeply against a rocky outcrop. A most essential companion should be a pocket book on the wild flowers of Scotland.

The glen is transformed by the dazzling yellow of the profusely flowering gorse during late spring to early summer. More commonly known as Whin in Scotland, the prickly Gorse (*Ulex europaeus*) flowers sometimes during a mild winter.

Continue to descend serene Gleann Oraid on the easy-going single-track road until you reach the tiny settlement under the shadow of Preshal More. Take the track on the left heading towards the bay lined by a stone wall, trees and woodland. The stone walls and woodland are a haven for mosses and lichens, a rare setting on Skye. The track eventually passes Talisker House dating from the 1720s, the favourite residence of the MacLeods after Dunvegan Castle.

More commonly known as Whin in Scotland, the prickly Gorse (*Ulex europaeus*) is profuse in flower during late spring and flowers sometimes during a mild winter. It grows freely throughout Skye, creating a cascade of dazzling yellow set against the rich green moorland of late spring through to early summer.

Dry stone wall Talisker. The growth of moss is aided by the expanse of trees at the foot of Gleann Oraid.

45

Low light over Talisker Bay creates an impression of monochrome.

Talisker Bay was described as unlike any other area of Skye in the writings of James Boswell. In 1773 Dr Johnson, along with James Boswell, while touring The Hebrides spent time at Talisker House. Boswell wrote of Talisker: 'Talisker is a better place than one commonly finds in Skye. It is situated in a rich bottom. Before it is a wide expanse of sea, on each hand of which are immense rocks; and, at some distance to the sea, there are three columned rocks rising to sharp points. The billows break with prodigious force and noise on the coast of Talisker. There are here a good many well grown trees.' The pair also spent time at Dunvegan Castle and Ullinish House. The previous year Thomas Pennant had completed his journey through the Highlands and Islands, and Dr Johnson said of Pennant that he was 'the best traveller ever read'.

A clear path continues over the waters running from Sleadale Burn following towering cliffs on your left until reaching the shore. The beach is made up of large pebbles and a fusion of white and black sand. The tall cliffs to the north are enhanced by a picturesque waterfall fed from Loch an Sguirr Mhoir. The beach, with its grassy foreshore, is a most pleasant place to rest and observe the 'billows breaking with prodigious force' before the return journey. As with most there-and-back walks, the scenery is equally magnificent as you take in the views that would have been missed on the outward journey, culminating with an easy-going steady climb back up through Gleann Oraid.

Talisker beach at low tide. The grey rocks and pebbles complement the combination of black and white sand.

47

Commanding views were afforded over Loch Bracadale from Dun Beag Broch, adding to the theory of their use as beacons by Martin Martin writing his account of his travels around The Hebrides.

Dun Beag Broch, Struan

Leaving Minginish behind, we now continue north, the A863 hugging the rugged coast for the majority of the next nine miles before reaching Struan, the journey providing spectacular views of the coast, and as we glimpse back south the distant Cuillin remain a prominent feature. Heading towards Struan, two distinctive landmarks, MacLeod's Tables, firstly come into view and will dominate most of our journey through north-west Skye. At Struan we find the remains of Dun Beag Broch, regarded as one of the best preserved on Skye. Derived from Norse *Borg*, meaning Fort, the broch was believed to have been built between 700 BC and AD 550. These massive dry stone structures were round in shape, with walls up to 12ft thick, and many can be found throughout the Western and Northern Isles.

Today the remaining walls are well preserved but would probably have stood up to 30ft high.

Massive blocks of stone were used in the construction of the dry stone walls, with the lower parts seemingly well preserved today.

The ground floor would almost certainly have been used for livestock, with the upper levels for living being roofed over with wood and thatch.

The structure would almost certainly have been roofed, with the stone stairs built inside the double layer of walls.

Dun Beag Broch was visited in 1772 by author of *A Tour In Scotland*, Thomas Pennant. Even today, their exact use is shrouded in mystery; some believe they were built solely for defence while others say they were used for habitation, being early farm houses.

Today, the remaining walls are well preserved but would probably have stood up to 30ft high, with the ground floor used for livestock and the upper levels for living being roofed over with wood and thatch. Commanding views are afforded over Loch Bracadale from Dun Beag Broch, adding to another theory of their use as beacons by Martin Martin, writing an account of his travels around The Hebrides during 1695. His book *A Description of the Western Isles of Scotland*, first published in 1703, is said to have aided future travellers such as Thomas Pennant, James Boswell and Samuel Johnson.

Massive blocks of stone were used in the construction of the dry-stone walls. During the years 1914 to 1920, Dun Beag was excavated, and it is debated that some rebuilding work could have taken place. Artefacts found during the excavations date from the Iron Age and Viking times.

A section of the stone stairs built inside the double layer of walls remains well preserved today.

Throughout Skye, derelict stone buildings and rusting tin roofs seem to harmonize with the rolling moorlands as they return back to the landscape.

A classic Highland scene on the shores of Loch Harport. The boat appears to have withstood all that Mother Nature has presented over many years nevertheless still appearing sea worthy and resolute.

Gentle burns surge after a spell of heavy rain to display powerful torrents and impressive waterfalls as they cascade seaward.

In June the long hours of daylight bestow spectacular midnight scenes. This tranquil view was taken from the shore across Loch Beag to Bracadale, a short distance from Dun Beag Broch.

Passing places on single-track roads are marked with a sign, but unless you want to make yourself very unpopular remember that these are passing and not parking places.

Duirinish

As we continue north to the rolling treeless moorlands and coastal fringes of Duirinish, the landscape becomes dominated by the mystifying flat-topped mountains of Healabhal Mhor standing over 1,530ft and the smaller-looking Healabhal Bheag, known locally and detailed on OS mapping as MacLeod's Tables.

On reaching Dunvegan, the remainder of the journey to the most westerly point on Skye takes us again over single-track roads. Driving these roads brings back memories of a bye-gone era but requires thought and concentration. There are usually plenty of passing places and these are marked with a sign, but unless you want to make yourself very unpopular remember that these are passing and not parking places. The trick on single-track roads is to drive with a combination of consideration and assertiveness. In an ideal world vehicles approaching one another should adjust their speeds so as to meet at a passing place, that way neither waits for the other, and both proceed at best speed.

Bear in mind that if the passing place is on the right and you reach it first, stop on the left side of the road opposite the passing place, do not be tempted into pulling across to the right. Another rule of the single-track road is not to let your concentration on what is coming the other way stop you keeping a close watch on your mirror. If someone comes up behind you they are travelling the road faster than you are, you should now use a passing place to pull over and let them through. This is more than simple courtesy, some of the road signs emphasise this point. The majority of single-track roads are unfenced and you will therefore find sheep and cattle at the side and on the road. Take particular care if you see a sheep on one side of the road and a lamb on the other; nine times out of 10 the lamb will run across the road to join its mother!

Enchanting light unfolds over Loch Dunvegan, with Healabhal Mhor and Healabhal Bheag silhouetted as the low winter sun beings to set.

MACLEOD'S TABLE WALK

Healabhal Mhor rises over 1,530ft above sea level, while the smaller in mass Healabhal Bheag rises above 1,600ft, both appearing as if they have been sliced off by a giant and legend claims just that. It is said they were sliced off to provide a bed and table for St Columba. Another legend has it that the ninth Chief of MacLeod wanted to impress Lords of the King's Court from Edinburgh so he invited them to a banquet at his 'room more lofty and a table more spacious' than they had, taking them to the flat-topped summit with light provided by his clansman, holding aloft flaming torches. The Lords were said to have been very impressed and spent some time at Dunvegan Castle. A less romantic view is that around 65 million years ago horizontal lava flows would have created these distinctive flat-topped hills.

MacLeod's Table North (Healabhal Mhor)

Distance 4.5 miles with an estimated time of 4.5 to 5 hours.

A walk to the summit of one of the dominate features of Duirinish, cloaked in myths and legends. The effort to negotiate the sometimes steep and pathless route is rewarded with truly magnificent views. Parking is roadside at grid reference 242 463 on the B884 single-track road from Dunvegan to Glendale.

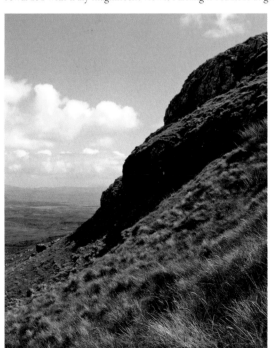

Begin with a short road walk back toward Dunvegan before taking the track on your right heading to the old settlement of Osdale appropriately named after Glen Osdale. Pass the refurbished cottages heading toward a burn, at this point the track deteriorates.

The burn can be crossed by negotiating stepping stones, but good footwear is advisable to ensure your feet remain dry. Beyond the burn the route now follows sheep tracks across the heather-clad moorland heading toward the distant summit. The moorland is a delight with many species of wild flower to be found, sometimes in abundance. As the summit gets closer, the slopes become much steeper and it does require selecting the easiest looking route, as there is no clear indication of the best line of ascent. Occasional ridges and outcrops of rock need to be overcome before reaching the base of the hill.

The steep upper slopes of Healabhal Mhor are in stark contrast to the mossy summit Plateau. During spring through to early summer, the slopes come alive with a superb display of wild flowers.

The Common Spotted Orchid grows in marshy boggy moorland, seen here on the upper slopes of Healabhal Mhor.

Looking west, high above Skinidin, with the views unfolding across Loch Dunvegan to the Coral Beaches and beyond.

The true base of the hill is a good place to rest a while and gaze in awe at the magnificent views with a chance to look back to the starting point to appreciate how much ascent has taken place.

The views to the north encompass Loch Dunvegan, the castle and the bright white sands of the Coral Beaches, Waternish and the distant Outer Hebrides. South east, the views overlook Loch Bracadale, and given the right weather conditions the distant Cuillin can also be seen. The final push to the flat-topped summit is very steep, mainly grassy, but as with the lower slopes you need to devise your own route. Keep well to the left of the steep cliffs that drop from the summit. Finally, the mossy plateau comes into view for the first time, unlike most hills and mountains where the destination for most of a walk is clearly visible. Head across the spongy flat-topped summit, keeping to the left of a lochan, to reach the large summit cairn where confirmation is gained that the flat-topped summit of Healabhal Bheag away to the south is indeed the loftier of the two.

After spending a considerable amount of effort reaching the flat summit, no one would question staying a fair while to admire the magnificent vista from the top. A circumnavigation of the entire summit is essential to appreciate the entire panorama, but take care as the summit's mosses can be very wet at times and boggy ground is treacherous and needs to be avoided. Be prepared for a breezy reception aloft, for even on the calmest of days the winds at the summit can be quite invigorating.

A large cairn marks the summit of Healabhal Mhor.

Officially called Harebell, this delicate flower is known as Bluebell in Scotland, flowering during mid-to-late summer.

The view from the summit of Healabhal Mhor leaves one in no doubt that the summit of Healabhal Bheag stands well above, merely 1.5 miles south. The furthest-most flat summit is Beinn na Boineid. The Minginish coast with the cliffs above Talisker Bay are visible in the far distance.

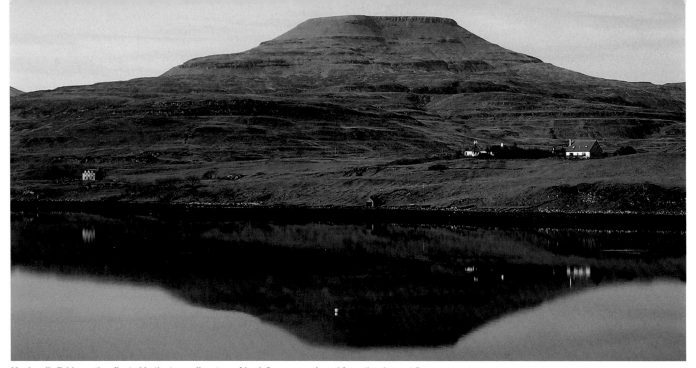

MacLeod's Table north reflected in the tranquil waters of Loch Dunvegan, viewed from the shore at Dunvegan.

The descent is taken by retracing your steps, again choosing your own route down, nevertheless made all the easier as you are now in full view of your destination. Although the walk to the summit and back looks reasonably easy, care needs to be taken as the upper slopes are very steep and may not be suitable for all. Mists can also descend rendering the upper slopes very dangerous. The distance is not great only four miles, but the going is hard at times; allow plenty of time for this walk to the lofty heights of Duirinish.

The single-track road continues north-westward where evidence of peat cutting can be seen. Peat cutting normally starts in May, taking advantage of the more clement summer weather to dry the peat. Cut into brick shapes using a tool known as a peat iron, the bricks are then laid across the moor to dry for about three weeks before being stacked and turned. The peat iron was designed to cut lift and throw the peat in one movement. Vast areas of Skye are covered in deep layers of peat that continue to grow each year. Crofters have a dedicated area of moor land where they are able to harvest the peat, used as household fuel in the Highlands for many centuries. Peat is formed in waterlogged, sterile acidic conditions that favour mosses, in particular sphagnum moss. As the plants die they are laid down and slowly build up as peat instead of decomposing due to the lack of oxygen in the bog.

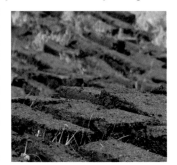

Working the peat bank.   **The peat laid out to dry.**

All that remains today of Kilchoan Church, one of the original parish churches on Skye, are the foundations and the graveyard.

Glendale

Glendale sits north west of Dunvegan accessible, only by the single-track road we are travelling along following the rugged shoreline of Loch Dunvegan, for most of the 10 miles a superb scenic journey. Glendale is made up from what are known as townships these being the small scattered settlements of Fasach, Feriniquarrie, Holmisdale, Lephin, Upper Milovaig, Lower Milovaig and Waterstein. The Glendale estate covers 23,000 acres, with its boundaries of Dunvegan in the east, Orbost in the south, and west to the Little Minch.

Close to The Hamara river lays the site of one of the original parish churches on Skye, Kilchoan Church. All that remains today are the foundations of this little church and the graveyard. The last service was said to have been held in the late 1700s. Tradition has it that the twisted elder tree that grows out of the little church was the site of the grave of a Scandinavian Prince known as Tiel, who came to grief in battle as his ship sailed into Loch Pooltiel, at that time known as Loch-a-Chuain.

At Holmisdale House you will find the Toy Museum, unique in that not all the toys are hidden behind glass. Different eras are represented, allowing one to rediscover memories that have long faded. A devastating fire in 2002 destroyed many of the original exhibits, but major rebuilding over the next 18 months saw the museum reopen, a fact that makes the range of toys on display all the more significant.

The Glendale Mill has now fallen into disrepair, the thatched roof having caved in.

At the head of Loch Pooltiel we find Glendale beach where the Hamara River flows into the sea having risen some six miles south east and 938ft high upon the slopes of Beinn a Chapuill in the shadow of Healabhal Mhor. A ruined watermill is evidence of past industrial activity at Glendale, where for centuries the islanders used water power to mill their flour. During the 1970s the mill was fully restored complete with replica machinery of the type that would have been used during its heyday. Sadly, it has now fallen into disrepair the thatched roof having caved in.

The wildlife of Loch Pooltiel is varied with minke whales, seals and otters all being spotted. The tall cliffs, together with its many waterfalls, provide a spectacular backdrop, especially when viewed from the coast below Lower Milovaig where access to the shoreline is easily obtained. During stormy weather and particularly after heavy rain, the waterfalls are literally blown back up the cliffs, producing a fascinating spectacle.

Glendale today is popular with tourists as the only route to Waterstein Head and Neist Point a further three miles west runs through Glendale. Many of the croft houses now serve as holiday accommodation for the growing tourist industry that caters for people seeking a holiday where you can find space and solitude among magnificent scenery.

The rusting cast-iron water wheel, showing signs of neglect.

A relic left over from past industrial activity.

A monument commemorates the Glendale Martyrs on the road to Glendale.

Ahead of Glendale are the scattered settlements of Upper and Lower Milovaig set on a promontory overlooking Loch Pooltiel. The loch is home to Meanish Pier, once a busy port with steamers arriving from South Uist and Glasgow bringing coal and other supplies to this remote part of Skye; we are now some 50 miles from the old ferry crossing at Kylerhea. Cattle boats used the pier as the dropping off point at the start of a Drovers trail across Skye. Before the coming of the single-track road, this rough track would have provided the only access into Glendale aside from the sea.

Today, one period in the history of the Highlands is still very emotive, the Highland Clearances. Whole crofting communities were cleared by the mainly absentee landlords who decided sheep were more profitable than the rents paid by the crofters. The clearance came later to Skye in comparison with other areas of the Highlands, but it is estimated that during the 1800s over 80,000 people were forced to leave their homes in the Highlands, shipped overseas to other continents. Throughout Skye you will find the scattered remains of derelict communities, croft houses razed to the ground still returning to Mother Nature, a lasting reminder of a turbulent period of Highland history.

One such area to the west of Upper Milovaig is Lorgill, set above the shore of Moonen Bay with a distressing secret past belying its present serenity.

Try to imagine a settlement of 10 families during the 1830s living in a small close-knit community seeking out a living from the land, having plentiful grazing for their livestock, the sea on their doorstep providing a rich harvest and fresh water from the burn, all the essential elements to maintain the family.

Suddenly and without warning they were forced from their homes, taking only what they could carry, marched overland 20 miles to Loch Snizort to be transported overseas to Nova Scotia. Anyone over the age of 70 was refused passage and would have been sent to Glasgow to see out their remaining days in the poor house. Their houses were subsequently razed to the ground rendering them derelict. The clearances continued well into the 19th century with the land given over to sheep and their tenant farmers transforming the Highlands into the landscape that we know today.

Glendale became famous in the early 1900s when crofters became freeholders of the land they worked and lived on. The Glendale Martyrs had campaigned for decades to achieve their aim, and some endured imprisonment during the late 1880s. Among them was John MacPherson, eventually leading an uprising against their landlord.

During the winter of 1883 a member of Glendale Estates trying to remove cattle was assaulted by the owners. Warrants were issued for their arrest with four policemen duly dispatched from Portree to Glendale. The police were met by a large crowd who subsequently overpowered them, hastening their retreat back to Portree. A Royal Navy gunboat docked at Meanish Pier to arrest MacPherson and four other crofters to stand trial. It was agreed that Lord Napier would set up a commission to look into the grievances of the crofters, taking evidence he recommended some reform. By this time, the Highland Land league was increasing in membership with feelings running high, and subsequent rent strikes were to become common place across the highlands and islands.

Prime Minister William Gladstone relented and eventually passed the Crofters Act of 1886, an act far more radical then Napier's reforms, giving the crofters security of tenure. The crofter's future was now secure with the croft passing to their heirs on death.

A memorial to the 'Glendale Martyrs' sits at the head of the Glendale road paying tribute to John MacPherson and his followers.

Loch Pooltiel from Milovaig.

Early morning at Meanish Pier on the shores of Loch Pooltiel,
now a small harbour for the farm fishing industry.

Close to Neist Point Waterstein Head towers 970ft above Moonen Bay. The head provides a plethora of changeable moods, at times showing its darker side, as storm clouds gather creating a sombre-looking Loch Mor in the foreground. Evidence of man's past activity can be clearly seen on the slopes above the loch.

WATERSTEIN HEAD WALK

Distance 2.5 miles, with an estimated time of 2–2.5 hours.

Waterstein Head stands proud among a chain of magnificent cliffs towering above the north-west coast of Duirinish in a line that extends for over 20 miles from Idrigill Point in the south culminating in the north at Biod an Athair, the tallest cliffs on Skye rising sheer from the shoreline to reach over 1,000ft above sea level. This stretch of coast is among the most magnificent to be found anywhere in the British Isles.

The walk, a relatively short one takes you to the trig point at the summit of Waterstein Head towering 970ft above Moonen Bay with superb views west across the Little Minch to the Outer Hebrides over 20 miles distant. MacLeod's Tables can be seen inland, and on a clear day views extend to the Cuillin. Moonen Bay was once fished by Gavin Maxwell, author of *Ring of BrightWater,* for Basking Sharks from his base on the small island of Soay off the south west of Skye close to Elgol. This is another there-and-back walk with a fairly steep ascent to a remote area of Skye offering a completely different view on the return journey, as you descend the turf hill views open up north to Biod an Athair (Skye Cliff) and the distant mountains of Harris.

Magnificent views begin to unfold as you gain height toward the summit of the Waterstein Head.

An eerie atmosphere of mystery and serenity surrounds the summit of Waterstein Head shrouded in sea mist 970ft above Moonen Bay.

The walk begins at grid reference 146 488, where you can park on the gravelled area just off the single-track road from Upper Milovaig. Leave the road heading down toward the escarpment edge with Loch Mor set out below following the remains of an old dyke (turf wall). This provides easy walking, making use of sheep tracks. The walk soon turns to a gentle climb, with views to Loch Mor opening up now far below on your right. Head slightly away from the dyke to find a gap in the old fence. Shortly after the fence, you head for a small ravine crossing the burn. Continue to follow the dyke as it climbs steeply, and eventually Waterstein Head comes into view in the distance beyond a slightly lower ridge.

During autumn the hill is home to a huge variety of brightly coloured Wax Cap fungi. Continue upward, where a rocky escarpment makes for a welcome place to sit and marvel at Neist Point and the lighthouse set out beneath, with the Outer Isles in the distance. (South Uist highest peaks Beinn Mhor over 2,000ft and Hecla appear remarkably close on a clear day are in fact 22 miles distant). On an overcast or misty day the outer Isles are hidden from view, but the walk should only be attempted when weather conditions are clear as the upper slopes follow close to a sheer drop.

Continue climbing upward, keeping on the grass above the cliff which at this point becomes steeper, now following a fence on your left. You will need to step over this fence and follow it upward, turning right to keep to the cliffs. To reach Waterstein Head go across to the top corner of the field where there is a trig point (997ft). To the south are views to the waterfalls of Ramasaig Cliff and the distant Hoe. Return by the same route, although the descent back to the car parking area is more leisurely than the climb, with the reward of distant views to the tallest cliffs on Skye across Loch Pooltiel to Biod an Athair.

Moonen Bay, Waterstein Head, Ramasaig cliffs and The Hoe.

Neist Point, the most westerly part of Skye, takes the full force of Atlantic storms when they first make landfall. The weather is in a changeable mood, with sunlight reflecting on the windswept sea. One such storm threatens but, as the saying goes, on Skye wait a while and the sun will shine again.

NEIST POINT WALK

Moonen Bay boasts some of the finest cliff scenery in Britain and Neist Point, our next destination, is no exception. There are two options for the starting point to this scenic coastal walk. The first is the parking area at the end of the single-track road directly above the escarpment overlooking Neist, the second and my preference would be to commence from the parking area at the beginning of the walk to Waterstein Head. Both of these walks could be done on the same day; in reality both deserve to be undertaken on different days to fully appreciate the magnificent scenery, allowing one time to seek out the flora and fauna. Seals, killer whales and occasional young basking sharks can be spotted at sea. The birdlife is astounding with meadow and rock pipit, common buzzard, rough-legged buzzard, golden eagle, eider and long-tailed ducks, and even occasional puffin have been spotted here while colonies of shags sit on the rocks far below the tall cliffs.

Distance 4.5 miles, with an estimated time of 3.5–4 hours.

The quiet single-track road makes for a pleasing stroll before descending the steep escarpment to Skye's most westerly point. Set off at grid reference 146 488 or the alternative shorter route at grid reference 132 478 at the end of the road.

Begin from the gravel parking area at grid reference 146 488 keeping to the road descending the steep hill to the scattered settlement of Waterstein, with Loch Mor set out below on your left. The road turns sharp left crossing a cattle grid beside the sheep pens. Stay on the single track road crossing another cattle grid where the views seaward become genuinely remarkable. On reaching the end of the road continue past the buildings at the top of the escarpment before steeply descending the steps on your left. There is no road access to Neist Point lighthouse and goods are taken down the steep incline by means of a hoist. If the hoist is operational take care, as the notice advises. Once past the winch at the foot of the steps continue through the gap crossing a wide grassy plateau before gaining height. The path follows the contours of the escarpment under the towering grassy slopes of An t–Aigeach, known locally as 'The Stallions Head'. On the seaward side the craggy rock face of An t-Aigeach rises 230ft sheer from the sea and is home to a colony of gannets.

The views to your left become awe-inspiring across the sweep of Moonen Bay. The panorama encompasses Waterstein Head gently yielding to Ramasaig Cliff, the cliffs in turn fall steeply to Ramasaig Bay before gaining height culminating at The Hoe. Since the opening of the Skye Bridge it has been said that Neist Point is nowadays the most westerly part of mainland Britain that one can access by road and on foot, some 13 miles further west than Land's End in Cornwall.

A colourful scene unfolds with the flowering of the heather-clad slopes.   **The sheer cliff face of An t-Aigeach becomes apparent when viewed from shore at Neist.**

67

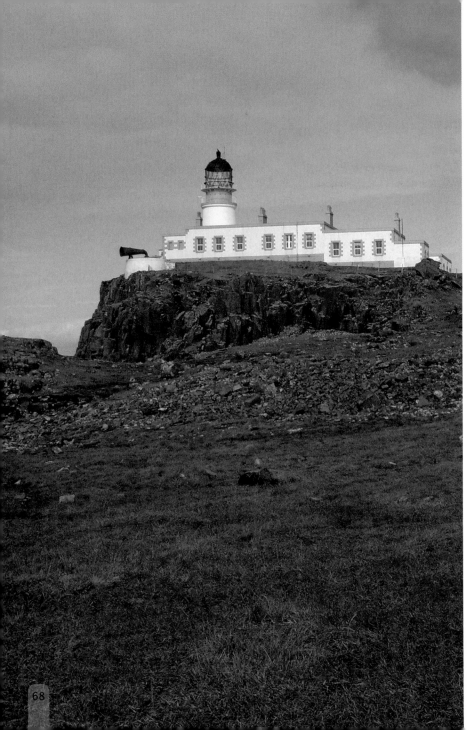

Neist Point lighthouse stands 62ft high, with the light set 142ft above the sea. Built in 1909, it was fully manned right up until 1990.

The lighthouse has to withstand the worst that nature can yield as the most severe of Atlantic winter storms first make landfall on Skye at Neist Point. Completed in 1909, the lighthouse was fully manned right up until 1990. The light is the equivalent of 480,000 candles and has a nominal range of 16 miles, but it is said to be visible for over 20 miles. The lighthouse stands 62ft high with the light set 142ft above the sea. In January 2005 the general lighthouse authorities came to a conclusion that the fog signal had a significantly reduced role in the modern marine environment, due to the use of electronic position finding aids and radar. The decision was taken that all fog horns were to be turned off, the last falling silent October 2005. Fog horns were first introduced to Scotland in 1876. When fog or mist rises the light becomes less visible and from a distance unseen. As with the light for identification, the sound from the fog horn was unique to the location.

The lighthouse buildings are now privately owned with no access available to the lighthouse. The walk to Neist Point has not always been straight forward as previous owners had restricted access to the path from the road.

The rock pools on the shore at Neist are home to sea anemones, carnivorous marine animals.

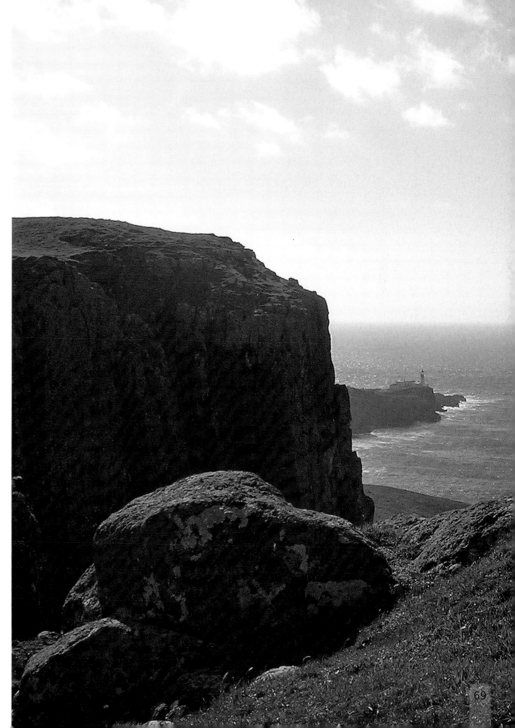

A short detour as you regain the road on the return part of the walk will present excellent views of Neist Point from the cliff path close to the old coastguard station.

Head for the jetty where numerous rock pools are teaming with aquatic life, including sea anemones, carnivorous marine animals that cling to the rocks. The reward for the effort is a small remote cove of white sand, similar to that found at the Coral Beaches, and black rocks pounded smooth by the relentless battering from Atlantic storms. Continue to the point rewarded with a view of Waterstein Head in the knowledge that you are now at the most westerly point of Skye. The return is by retracing the outward journey, but a detour along the northern cliff edge will provide you with magnificent views back to the lighthouse and the sheer cliff face of An t-Aigeach, with a chance to get a closer look at the colony of gannets. Take care, as the exposed cliff face drops steeply away.

Continue across the grassy plateau, where once the lighthouse keepers would play golf, to reach the winch house. To rejoin the road from here requires a steep climb. A good excuse for a rest on the climb up the numerous steps is to look back and marvel at the panorama of Neist set out below with distant views to the outer isles. Continue following the road, crossing a cattle grid before passing the scattered settlement of Waterstein with views to the escarpment of Druim nan Sgarbh ahead. Cross the second cattle grid where the road bears sharp right before the final push up the steep incline to the parking area overlooking Loch Mor.

As with most of Skye's promontories, our journey now continues by retracing the single-track road that brought us to our latest destination. Early travellers would describe this area beyond Glendale as being at the ends of the earth as the next landfall due west is America.

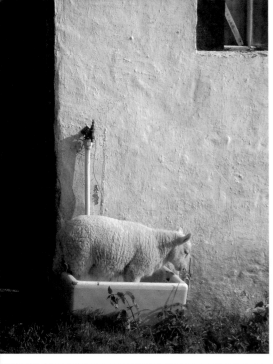

Baa-th time. During late spring to early summer Skye becomes home to numerous new-born lambs. They are a constant source of amusement, exploring their natural and sometimes man-made surroundings.

The moment when a new day dawns. The morning sky transformed with an explosion of light as the sun rises above the distant Red Cuillin, reflecting in the still waters of Loch Dunvegan. The ebbing tide leaving pools of water shimmering amid the rocky shore, adding to a most magical early morning feel of serenity.

Some sheep are on the pitch; they think it's all over, it is now! Taken on Cup Final day, well at least it was at Hampden Park and Wembley. You could not get much further removed from the hustle and bustle of those famous sporting events than here at Glendale. The legendary comments from the late Kenneth Wolstenholme back in 1966 are slightly changed for the occasion, and by the look of the goal posts they may well have been last painted back then.

The tranquil shores of Loch Dunvegan are to be our close companion for the next 12 miles as the single-track road skirts the scenic loch for most of the return journey to Dunvegan, the seat of Clan MacLeod. High above Dunvegan stands Duirinish Millennium Stone, erected by the people of Dunvegan to mark the year 2000. Taken from the shore of Strathaird in the south of Skye, the stone was transported using the same techniques that would have been used thousands of years ago. The stone was brought by boat then raised into position using manpower and wooden A frames. Standing 15ft high and weighing five tons, the stone is set high above the old church at Dunvegan with commanding views to MacLeod's Tables and the distant Cuillin.

The mirrored waters of Loch Dunvegan create a tranquil scene, providing the best opportunity for spotting otters feeding along the water's edge.

Duirinish Millennium Stone, erected by the people of Dunvegan to mark the year 2000.

Dunvegan Castle

According to their own genealogies, the MacLeods and Dunvegan became intertwined in the 13th century through the marriage of their progenitor, Leod, with the heiress of the Macarailts, in those days the Viking Seneschals of Skye who lived at Dunvegan. Leod himself was a son of Olaf the Black, King of the Isle of Man, who in turn was descended from the Norse king Harald Hardrada. Leod and his Lady had two sons, Tormod and Torquil, progenitors respectively of the MacLeods of Dunvegan, Harris and Glenelg and the MacLeods of Lewis. The gaelic word *Mac*, meaning 'son of' helps to symbolise the moment when Clan MacLeod first appears as a historical reality.

Among all the historic houses of Scotland, there is none that for sheer manifold fascination overtops Dunvegan Castle. It is at once the greatest and most renowned among Hebridean strongholds, and the only one which has been continuously owned and (with the exception of the 80 years after the Potato Famine of the 19th century) occupied by the same family, during a period now reaching back over a span of very nearly eight centuries. Architecturally, it is a structure of high importance, containing work of at least 10 building periods. Its history, and that of the famous clan whose chiefs have ruled from their castled rock during all these many generations, is rich with drama and packed with colourful interest.

Within Dunvegan's stately halls are priceless heirlooms, some of which have descended in the hands of the chiefs of MacLeod since mediaeval times.

The castle is situated on an upstanding mass of partly columnar basalt, approximately 30ft high, arising from the shores of Loch Dunvegan. Around it originally the sea ebbed and flowed. An important feature which gave Dunvegan Castle and those within its great strength was the existence of a fresh-water well. With this priceless resource added to the impregnability of its position, Dunvegan Castle presented a formidable obstacle to the enemies of the chiefs of Clan Macleod.

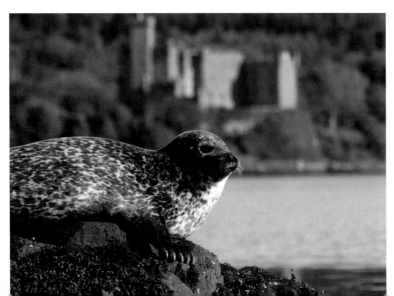

Nature and man-made in harmony.

The magnificent stronghold of Clan MacLeod reflected in the still waters of the loch.

The Fairy Flag; was it the robe of an early Christian saint or the war banner of Harold Hardrada, King of Norway, killed in 1066, or did it emerge mysteriously from some grassy knoll in Skye?

Legends, however fantastic or far-fetched they may appear to be, are rarely without some trace of historical fact.

When a relic survives to tell its own story, that at least is one fact that is impossible to ignore. The precious Fairy Flag of Dunvegan, the most treasured possession of the clan, is just such a relic. The traditional tales about its origin, some of them very old indeed, have two themes – Fairies and Crusaders. Fairy stories are difficult to relate to fact; they often occur as a substitute for forgotten truth. The connection with the Crusades can, however, be linked to the only definite information available as to the origin of the Fairy Flag – the fabric, thought once to have been dyed yellow, is silk from the Middle East (Syria or Rhodes); experts have dated it between the 4th and 7th centuries, in other words, at least 400 years before the First Crusade. So was it the robe of an early Christian saint? Or the war banner of Harold Hardrada, King of Norway, killed in 1066, or did it emerge mysteriously from some grassy knoll in Skye? The legends are all we have to guide us to the answer.

'The Crusader version'.

A Macleod on a crusade to the Holy Land received food and shelter from a hermit in a dangerous mountain pass on the borders of Palestine. The Hermit warned him that an evil spirit, a destroyer of true belief, guarded the pass, but that with some advice and a piece of the True Cross he might get through. The MacLeod slew the spirit, The Daughter of Thunder, *Nein na Pheupere* him the future of his clan, directing him to take her girdle and make a banner of it and to make a staff of her spear.

'The Fairy Bridge version'.

Once upon a time a fairy married a MacLeod chief and was permitted to remain with him for 20 years before returning to fairyland. When the sad day came to part, the chief took leave of his wife at the Fairy Bridge 3 miles from Dunvegan. She gave him the Banner, telling him that when he was hard pressed in battle, waving it would bring a host of armed men to his side.

Rory Mor's Horn.

Bonnie Prince Charlie

Although the Chief at the time of the '45 did not support Bonnie Prince Charlie, many of his clan did do so.

Visible from the castle on the other side of the Loch is Galtrigal, the home of the prince's pilot, Donald MacLeod of Galtrigal, the man who brought the prince 'Over the sea to Skye' from Uist during the time when he was a fugitive. At the time the chief was one of the people searching to apprehend the prince. Flora MacDonald, the Jacobite heroine, was in the boat with the Prince, and equally being hunted by the MacLeod chief.

By one of those quirks of fate, some 20 or 30 years later, her daughter had married the tutor to the young Chief of MacLeod, and was living in the castle. The mother, on one of her return visits from America where she had emigrated, is believed to have stayed for two or three years in the castle and left her personal Jacobite relics to her daughter.

Within Dunvegan's stately halls are priceless heirlooms, some of which have descended in the hands of the chiefs of MacLeod since mediaeval times. The Dunvegan Cup is one such heirloom believed to date from AD 900, given to Rory Mor by the O'Neills of Ulster for services rendered during their wars with Queen Elizabeth I of England in 1595.

Thus you will see in the castle still today her stays, her pin-cushion with the names of those who suffered in the '45, a lock of the prince's hair, a list of her children, and a small portrait of herself copied by the wife of the 24th chief. Exhibited in the castle are also the spectacles of Donald MacLeod of Galtrigal, the prince's boatman, and the Amen Glass which was given to Donald MacLeod by the prince, inscribed with the words 'To my faithful Palinurus', alluding to the boatman who conducts people across the Loch. Another interesting object with a fanciful engraving of the prince is the tooth of a sperm whale, which can also be seen in the castle today.

The Clan MacLeod has survived down the centuries, surviving the extremes of feast and famine, the intermittent periods of warring with neighbouring clans, and the immense changes of social, political and economic life through which the Western Highlands and Islands have passed.

Although three individual chiefs in the last seven generations have been comprehensively ruined by the apocalyptic difficulties caused by the unrelenting hostility from centralised government towards the clan system practised behind the Highland line, the chief and his clans folk have remained faithful to Dunvegan Castle and the rock on which it stands.

The 27th chief was the first chief to share his home with the public by opening it for charitable purposes two days a week in 1933. Since then the number of visitors has risen from a few hundred to tens of thousands.

One of the many relics from the past on display at the castle.

'A visit to Dunvegan Castle provides one with an altogether fascinating and memorable experience.'

The sunsets on Skye are a truly spectacular sight, but the sun rise should not be overlooked even though it can sometimes instigate an early start. The winter sun rises over Loch Dunvegan, creating a shimmering surface with the majestic Cuillin in the distance complementing the scene. The summits of the Black Cuillin and the more rounded tops of the Red Cuillin are clear to see.

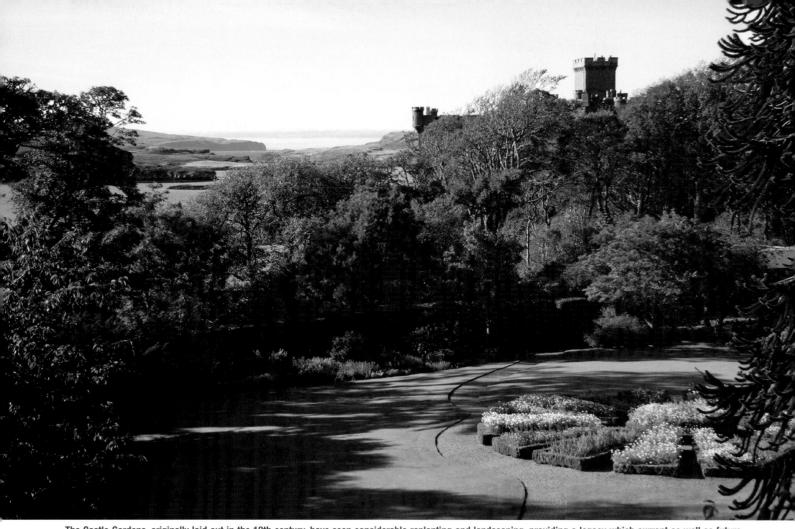

The Castle Gardens, originally laid out in the 18th century, have seen considerable replanting and landscaping, providing a legacy which current as well as future generations can enjoy and admire.

The Castle gardens lie inland and are backed by mature woodlands. As the Isle of Skye is essentially made up of barren treeless moorland, these woods and gardens are like reaching a hidden oasis. The magnificent gardens provide considerable interest to many, following paths through woodland glades, past shimmering pools and burns fed by a cascading waterfall.

The Castle Gardens were originally laid out in the 18th century, and considerable replanting and landscaping provides a legacy which current as well as future generations can enjoy and admire.

Uiginish Point with a backdrop of the lower slopes of Beinn Chreagach. The light from the beacon has a range of 7 miles.

The tranquil waters of Loch Dunvegan are home to many islets, small uninhabited islands, and the knoll at Uiginish, its highest point a mere 140ft above sea level. Uiginish Point is home to Uiginish beacon, a white plain structured tower just 16ft high. The light flashes white, red, green every three seconds and can be seen from as far away as the Little Minch beyond Dunvegan Head, a distance of some 7 miles. Colonies of seals thrive on these uninhabited islets, and if you are lucky and the waters are calm you may just spot an otter or two.

Bonnie Prince Charlie had to leave Skye in a hurry, but you can stay for as long as you like to enjoy the varied wildlife of Loch Dunvegan and the spectacular views of the Outer Hebrides across the Little Minch. Seal boat trips depart from the pier below Dunvegan Castle using traditionally built clinker boats to visit the seal colony, where you can observe these playful sea mammals at close quarters. The knowledge of the boat men is second to none and you may see herons nesting as well as many other species of birds, including the arctic tern and the magnificent sea eagle.

The tranquil waters of the loch were in the past busy with steamers arriving at Dunvegan, once the main port to the Western Isles during the 1890s, with the last steamers departing during the 1950s.

Common Seals

Loch Dunvegan provides a safe haven for a colony of common seals. The waters of the loch are shallow enough to prevent whales entering allowing the seals to bask in peace between feeding.

The seals will leave the sanctuary of the loch on the rising tide to feed in the fish-rich deeper waters of the Little Minch, returning to rest for several hours before setting out again to feed. Common seals have their pups during June, unlike the Atlantic seals who give birth during autumn. The seals are a delight to watch, some becoming stranded with the ebbing tide on the higher rocks having to wait several hours for the tide to turn, before re-entering the water. Common seals are furry and can be seen leaping out of the water, much like a dolphin, to assist the fundamental process of moulting.

The shallow waters of the loch are a haven for wildlife, and a little further north from here are the means of support for the wonderful manifestation of the Coral Beaches.

The loch provides an opportunity for an intimate look at the colonies of common seals resting between forays into the Little Minch. Over 90 per cent of the British population of common seals, also known as harbour seals, are to be found in Scotland. They give birth ashore to their pups in June. Resting periods between feeding at sea ensure the common seals can be seen hauled upon the rocks of the tiny islets in a pattern reflecting the changing tides. The common seals seen here on Loch Dunvegan feed further out to sea before returning on the ebbing tide to rest upon the rocks, nourished on a variety of prey including sand eels, whitefish, herring, sprat and occasional octopus.

The fine white sand of the Coral Beaches is not true coral but come from the bleached exoskeletons of the red seaweed Lithothanium Calcareum. The Coral Beaches are only accessible via the path from Claigan.

CORAL BEACHES WALK

Distance 4 miles, with an estimated time of 3 hours.

A short coastal walk promising excellent views, leading to the bright white sands of the Coral Beaches. The walk starts at Claigan a remote group of crofts at the end of the single-track road leading north west from Dunvegan. From the car park, the walk follows a track that gradually approaches the shore, first passing the small bay of Camas Ban. In bright sunshine the sands of the Coral Beaches are startlingly white, giving an illusion of a tropical island set against the azure sea.

This most gentle of walks begins at the car park grid reference 232 537. Pass through the kissing gate to follow a good track across a field. After a spell of wet weather the burn will need to be negotiated, but several stones make crossing easy. Pass through another gate to follow the track down to the shore. The small bay of Camas Ban is the first Coral Beach to be seen. I have heard it said that some visitors have thought this to be their destination, although at times of high tide very little of the beach is visible.

Easy walking is provided on the track from Claigan to Camas Ban, the first Coral Beach.

83

A close inspection reveals the intricate shapes and make up of the bright white Coral Beaches.

Carry on bearing slightly away from the coast to cross another burn, heading upward to a gap in the wall. A clear path continues, where in a short distance you are rewarded with the superb views to the main coral beach; if you have chosen a sunny day the azure seas and the bright white sands give an illusion of a tropical paradise. Continue on towards the beach with easy walking over short turfs. On reaching the beach you will find that the sand is not true coral but comes from the bleached exoskeletons of the red seaweed Lithothanium Calcareum which grows in the shallow waters off shore. The red seaweed lays down an exoskeleton of chalk; when alive it is pink but becomes bleached white when dead.

The steep sided Cnoc Mor Ghrobain that rises behind the beach is worth a climb, a mere 65ft, a modest ascent compared to Skye's other coastal features, however your reward is a fine viewpoint. Dunvegan Head across Loch Dunvegan is clear to see, as are MacLeod's Tables and the distant outer isles. During the summer months wildflowers are abundant on the grassy slopes and rocky outcrops of Cnoc Mor Ghrobain. Having spent time admiring the views, move down to the shore and continue on around the rocky headland to Groban na Sgeire. To the north lie the Islands of Isay and Mingay. The wall running to the sea can be followed for a short distance, making use of sheep tracks above the rugged coast to view Lovaig Bay. Stein on the coast of Waternish is a mere 2.5 miles across the bay; however, due to the characteristics of Skye's peninsulas to reach Stein necessitates a 14-mile road journey back via Dunvegan. The topography does, though, provide for an exceptionally picturesque coastal journey.

Cnoc Mor Ghrobain affords splendid views south to MacLeod's Tables, west to Dunvegan Head and north east to Waternish. A modest climb of 65ft compared to Skye's other coastal features, but the reward is well worth the effort.

A good walking companion on Skye during late spring to early summer has to be a Scottish wild flower pocket guide book, to help identify the infinite variety of wild flowers. The plants growing at the Coral Beaches with the bright yellow flower heads I am advised are Common Birdsfoot-trefoil. The yellow flowers are streaked with red when in bud. Looks like it could be!

Wild flowers gain a precarious foothold on the rocky outcrop of Cnoc Mor Ghrobain.

The way back to the car park at Claigan is by retracing your steps, but why not spend some considerable time just sitting on the rocks or the beach listening to the shallow waters of Loch Dunvegan tumbling over the durable coral. On the return a slight deviation follows the rocky headland back to the main track. Keep to the seaward side where the path begins to rise as you leave the relatively flat foreshore, rejoining the track on the other side of the wall at Camas Ban. From here, follow the outward track back to the car park with views across Loch Dunvegan to the unmistakable MacLeod's Tables.

To continue our journey we now find ourselves travelling back through Dunvegan, all the while keeping a watchful eye on the loch, particularly if conditions are flat calm, the best opportunity to spot otters along the shore, feeding among the kelp. The next destination Waternish, Skye's smallest peninsula, is home to the oldest inn on Skye and the site of one of the most infamous of clan battles.

Nature displays a wonderful show of flora during the summer months, advantaged by the long hours of daylight at this latitude. Among the diverse selection are to be found the free flowering sea campion.

The bright white sands of the Coral Beaches on a glorious sunny day; this could be anywhere in the Caribbean, aside from the temperature being a lot more comfortable at this latitude.

The Inn at Stein.

Waternish

One of Skye's smallest peninsulas, Waternish has a turbulent history, one involving clan feuds, massacres, and a significant period of depopulation resulting from the Highland Clearances. The peninsula is home to the oldest inn on Skye; the Stein Inn dating from the late 18th century.

Stein, nestling on the shores of Loch Bay, is a tiny hamlet accessed only by a single-track road that wends its way down to the sea.

The most spectacular of sunsets unfold before you enhanced by the magnificent backdrop across Loch Bay of the small island of Isay, Ardmore Point and beyond to the Outer Hebrides, at times appearing remarkably close.

Stein was originally built during the late 1700s as a fishing village, complete with houses for the fisherman and a pier. For a while it became the busiest fishing village on Skye, but it seemed that the settlers could survive by living off the land, without having the need to spend time at sea. Now a picturesque seaside village, Stein was home for a while to the famous 1960s singer Donovan.

As we leave yet another magical place our next destination takes us to one with a gruesome past, just over 4 miles north west we come to the ruined church at Trumpan.

The Stein Inn sign reveals the effect of salt water nestled as it does on the shores of Loch Bay.

The bright orange Montbretia bring a splash of contrasting colour during late summer to the shores of Loch Bay.

The sunsets on Skye are truly spectacular and long lasting, perhaps none more so that here on Waternish. The view above Stein encompasses Loch bay, Ardmore Point the islands of Clett, Mingay and the distant mountains of North Uist and Harris silhouetted against a dramatic sky.

Beyond Trumpan there is nothing but cliffs and open moorland, apart from a small unmanned lighthouse at Waternish Point. There is a true feeling of remoteness about the promontory, although this has not always been so. The ruined crofts at Unish bear witness to the infamous Highland Clearances, and clan battles are commemorated along the coast. A Cairn was built as a memorial to Roderick Macleod of Unish who died during one such clan battle around 1530 between the MacDonalds of Trotternish and the MacLeods.

It has been said that this is where Skye meets the sky, and with the extremely clear air at times the Outer Hebrides running in an arch for over 130 miles north to south feel almost within reach, even though they are more than 25 miles distant.

Bonnie Prince Charlie, aided by Donald MacLeod and Flora Macdonald while escaping from South Uist, landed near Waternish Point. It is said that here they rested a while before continuing having been thwarted in an attempt to land at Ardmore Point, where during a storm they were fired upon by soldiers.

Trumpan Old Church

It is here at Trumpan that perhaps one of most cruel events in the island's sometimes brutal and bloody past was carried out at Trumpan Old Church. Trumpan's place in history was earned as a result of two massacres on the same day, a Sunday in May 1578.

The chain of events had begun the previous year when Clan MacLeod found almost 400 MacDonalds hiding in a cave on the Isle of Eigg; the MacLeods suffocated them by entrapping them in the cave then setting fire to the entrance.

On that fateful Sunday in 1578 the MacDonalds arrived from Uist by boat at Ardmore Bay below Trumpan. Under a veil of mist they came ashore unnoticed, moving to barricade the local population in the church. Seeking revenge for the massacre on Eigg they set fire to the thatched roof. The consequences of their actions resulted in the death of the entire congregation, aside from a small girl, who managed to escape to raise the alarm.

Clan MacLeod arrived swiftly from Dunvegan where the flames had been seen to seek out revenge, and the MacDonalds never returned to Uist. Capturing the boats that by now were stranded in Ardmore Bay on an ebbing tide, they attacked and killed the MacDonalds, lining them up next to a turf dyke. The turf and stone wall was pushed over burying their bodies. To this end, the Battle of Trumpan is also referred to as the battle of the spoiled dyke.

The graveyard and ruins of Trumpan Church lie toward the end of the Waternish peninsula above Ardmore Bay, one of the most tranquil parts of Skye.

Portree

Our brief visit to Waternish ends back at the famous Fairy Bridge, and we now head east, passing below the slopes of Ben Aketil, the site of the first wind farm on Skye. As we continue through several small settlements, the original single-track road is still visible at times to our left. On reaching Borve we turn right for a short distance to arrive at Portree, the island's capital. Portree takes its name from the Gaelic (*Port-an-Righ*) meaning King's Port, named after the visit by King James V in 1540 on his visit to the Highlands in an attempt to quell the clan battles of the time, although there is some dispute to this theory. Prior to this, the settlement was known as Kiltaraglen. Bonnie Prince Charles bade farewell to Flora MacDonald for the last time from Portree, while he was staying at The Royal Hotel, formerly MacNabs Inn.

The harbour, once used by steamers in the 1850s, is today used for fishing boats and pleasure craft.

In 1771 Portree had been developed as a fishing port by Sir James Macdonald. The port has witnessed numerous sad farewells, with countless sailings away from Skye particularly after the infamous potato famine of 1846 and the subsequent Highland Clearances that continued for the remainder of the late 1800s. During his visit to Skye in 1773, James Boswell made note that Mrs Mackinnon told him 'Last year when the ship sailed from Portree for America the people on shore were almost distracted when they saw their relations go off: they lay down on the ground and tumbled and tore the grass with their teeth. This year there was not a tear shed. The people on shore seemed to think they would soon follow.'

The natural setting for the harbour is enhanced by the coastal scenery and views to the Cuillin. Today used for fishing boats and pleasure craft, it was once used by steamers in the 1850s for several destinations including Glasgow and Stornoway. The brightly painted cottages that line the harbour have been featured on many calendars over the years similar to the famous harbour side of Tobermory.

Located on the southern outskirts of Portree you will find the Aros Centre, Skye's visitor centre which includes an innovative exhibition on the history of the island from 1700.

Brightly painted cottages adorn the harbour side at Portree.

The quayside.

Note the flap on the letter box to keep the elements out.

Trotternish

Leaving behind the island capital, we now take the main A87 heading once again north to the most mystifying and surreal of Skye's peninsulas, Trotternish. The largest landslip to have occurred in Britain has created a 20 mile inland cliff, the Trotternish Ridge.

We skirt the waters of Loch Snizort Beag, a loch that saw numerous sad farewells from these shores during the Highland Clearances. We pass Kingsburgh where Bonnie Prince Charlie spent the night having earlier landed on Skye close to Monkstadt with Flora MacDonald.

As the main port of Uig comes into view all is not as it seems. Overlooking Uig Bay at South Cuil we find resembling a Norman Tower, Captain Fraser's folly dating from the 1890s. It is said the captain was a notorious landlord and the folly was once used as a collection point for the crofters to pay their rent. The tower is now empty, no longer inhabited since the 1950s, although plans are under way to restore the tower for residential use once again.

Below is the small port of Uig, the ferry terminal to Lochmaddy, North Uist and Tarbert on the Isle of Harris. Before reaching the port, a single-track road on our right begins to climb, negotiating a hair-pin bend to reach a fork in the road. The right fork would take us across the backbone of Trotternish to reach the ridge, while the left will skirt the west coast to reach Kilmuir the location of the Skye Museum of Island life and Duntulm, home to a ruined castle, our two next ports of call.

The Blackface sheep is today the most common hill breed in Scotland, introduced into North Scotland in the early 19th century. Blackfaces are horned, with a black or black-and-white face and legs. Cheviot sheep whose wool was more valuable took their place for a while but now more popular as they can survive in the harsh climate of the hills and mountains of Scotland.

Appearing to date from Norman times, Captain Fraser's folly was in fact built during the 1890s.

Memorial to Flora
MacDonald, Kilmuir.

Kilmuir

At Kilmuir we seem to have travelled back in time as we approach a crofting settlement from the 19th century; it is in fact the Skye Museum of Island Life. Before visiting the museum, we continue a short distance past the entrance to perhaps the most iconic tribute on Skye, a monument to the memory of Flora MacDonald.

Flora was staying with her uncle on South Uist in the Outer Hebrides when Bonnie Prince Charlie sought refuge after fleeing from the defeat at Culloden. With a huge bounty on his head, time was running out for Charlie who, having been tracked down to Uist, Flora agreed to help smuggle the Prince to Skye, dressed as her maid Betty Burke. They set off in an open boat running into a storm off Ardmore Point, coming under fire from soldiers they were forced to find shelter for a while in a cave at Waternish Point, eventually arriving at Monkstadt, spending one night at Kingsburgh ahead of reaching Portree a day later. As they parted the Prince gave Flora a lock of his hair, she kept one of the sheets that the Prince had slept in later to be used as her shroud.

Flora was arrested and imprisoned for a while in the Tower of London for her help in Prince Charlie's escape but released under the Act of Indemnity 1747, later marrying Allan MacDonald of Kingsburgh in 1750. Sailing to live in America in 1774, Flora eventually returned to Skye after the War of Independence. Flora died in 1790. It is said that 3,000 mourners attended the funeral. The Celtic cross in the graveyard at Kilmuir was erected in 1880 and engraved are the words of Dr Johnson.

FLORA MACDONALD Preserver of PRINCE CHARLES EDWARD STUART
'Her name will be mentioned in history and if courage and fidelity be virtues, mentioned with honour.'

Skye Museum of Island Life. Kilmuir.

The museum is built around a reconstructed small crofting village, on display almost everything that such a township on Skye would have contained over a century ago.

Skye Museum of Island Life

A hundred years ago thatched houses were very much a part of the Highland scene and within their walls, by the light of the peat fire, the crofters of the Islands kept alive the songs and stories which have made the Hebrides famous throughout the world. Warm, sturdy and economical of scarce materials, the croft house was admirably suited to the landscape and the climate. It embodied the principles of streamlining hundreds of years before scientists thought of the idea, with the result that it could stand up to the worst of winter gales. As their numbers fast diminish, it is appropriate that a few should be preserved; and it was with this in mind that a group of old thatched buildings was set aside as a museum.

The first cottage to be opened to the public in 1965 was the dwelling house, which dates back to the mid-19th century. This cottage is a good example of the typical Skye house of that era, when houses on the island, with very few exceptions, were of this standard and type. By present-day standards the old Highland house was basic and crude but nevertheless, it was adequate in its own day and gave shelter and warmth to men and women who spent most of their time out of doors and cared little about worldly possessions or domestic luxury.

Part of the exterior display.

The interiors of the croft houses are complete with many important relics from Skye's history.

When a house was being planned, the first requisite was the finding of a suitable stance and, needless to say, a spot near a well was preferred since all the water for the household had to be carried by hand in buckets. The availability of stones was also a major consideration, and if enough stone could not be found near at hand the sitting of the house could suffer. On a treeless island such as Skye, the finding of suitable timber for the roof could also present a problem. Driftwood was often all that could be found. Before the era of lighthouse development and in the days of wooden ships, shipwrecks were quite a common occurrence, often providing a Godsend, as timber in abundance was cast upon the shores.

The type of cottage to be found on Skye was built with walls up to three feet in width and beating a hip-ended roof with over-hanging eaves of thatch, which formed a fringe around the wall top. The roof was constructed on the couple and purlin system, with rafters of rough, round timber. Light branches laid neatly over the purlins carry the 'divots' or turf squares which were neatly tiled to form a bed for the thatch. The thatch used on Skye was common rush or locally grown reeds.

As one enters the croft house (the largest in the group) the room to the right is the kitchen, and here the family cooked, ate and sat – it was the main room in the house. All the cooking was done on the peat fire which burned day and night, summer and winter on the open hearth. Heavy pots of cast iron were used, and the three-legged pot was often to be suspended over the flame by means of the 'swee'.

The cruise, a lamp burning fish liver oil was used before paraffin lamps became common. The crockery in the home was displayed on the shelves of the dresser and it was customary to display coronation memorabilia and other artefacts on a prominent shelf. The furniture consisted mainly of a bench or settle, a table, a barrel chair by the fireside for the 'man of the house', and another two or three chairs or stools for the family or the visitor.

On a mantelpiece one would always find a Gaelic bible and a family photograph if such was available. No Highland cottage was complete without a set of bagpipes, a fiddle or a Jew's harp. These items were indeed necessities, as crofting families had to depend entirely on their own resources.

The father was often able to teach his sons the art of playing some instrument, and how better could one pass a winter evening than in the happy atmosphere of Gaelic songs, music and discussion around a cosy peat fire? There can be few parts of the world, if any, which have such a wide and varied culture as the Highlands and Islands of Scotland, and in their language, song and music they have a great deal of which to be proud.

The kitchen was the main room of the croft house.

The Ceilidh House

The word *Ceilidh* means a small homely gathering of friends.

Before the arrival of radio and television, it was customary for neighbours to meet together during the long winter evenings to make their own entertainment. Songs were sung, stories were told and discussion on many and varied topics took place. Young and old engaged in the congenial proceedings, and as they sat happily around the peat fire the long dark night soon wore away, leaving with each and all a sense of the close community spirit and atmosphere, that was once so characteristic of the islands of the Hebrides.

James Boswell, in an account of his visit to Skye along with Dr Johnson in 1773, describes a house in which they stayed in south Skye. He states: 'We had no rooms that we could command, for the good people here had no notion that a man could have any occasion but for a mere sleeping place.'

The bellows would have been used to ensure the peat fire burnt continually, day and night, winter and summer.

The smithy could be found in every community, a very popular meeting place for the local folk.

The Old Smithy

A smithy could be found in every community in the past, but today the function is no longer required in rural crofting areas, as mechanisation has long since taken over from the good and faithful workhorse. The smithy was a very popular meeting place for the local folk, young and old alike. The smith was never to be found alone, and all the happenings of the place were discussed in his hearing by those who called in.

In the Islands, farriery was the mainstay of the smith's income. Every crofter had a horse, or sometimes two, and in the busy seasons of spring and summer there was always a horse in the smithy being shod. In winter the smith was never idle and was always at his anvil making horseshoes or mending the many various items sent to him for repair.

The Weaver's Cottage

The small cottage could often be seen as a very busy workshop. The village weaver could always find plenty of work to keep the shuttle going, producing not only the tweed for all types of garments but also for blankets and plaids. The old handloom on display at the museum is over 100 years old and is typical of the type used in homes of the Highlands before automatic looms were introduced. The old barn completes the crofting community.

Leaving the past behind, we head north east to Duntulm, our journey taking us through a dramatic boulder-strewn landscape below the 300ft towering mass of Bealach Lochdarach, travelling along a rugged sweep of coastline.

The weaver's house.

A cairn commemorates the MacArthurs who were pipers to the MacDonalds.

DUNTULM CASTLE TO RUBHA HUNISH WALK

Distance 4.75 miles, with an estimated time of 3 hours.

A spectacular coastal walk draped with a turbulent history, visiting the ruined castle at Duntulm and the abandoned township of Erisco. The walk takes you above the northern-most point of Skye, Rubha Hunish, a remote promontory made more so as the only access is by negotiating the precarious descent of the 300ft-high cliffs of Meall Tuath guarding over the headland. The route to this northern most point begins following the rocky shoreline with the return taking advantage of the distant views to the Trotternish Ridge from the heather clad hillsides above the abandoned crofts of Erisco.

Park on the roadside close to the castle at grid reference 410 740. A visit to the ruined castle is probably best taken before the walk as most of the route can be seen from the castle walls. Go through the gate to reach the castle sat proudly on a rocky promontory overlooking Tulm Bay. Once an Iron Age broch the site of Duntulm Castle has also been used as a Viking stronghold before being occupied by the MacLeods in the 14th century.

Little remains of the original castle.

104

Once an Iron Age broch, the site of Duntulm Castle has also been used as a Viking stronghold before being occupied by the MacLeods in the 14th century.

The castle was later inhabited by the MacDonalds, who were known as the Lords of the Isles. The MacDonalds enlarged the structure during the 17th century.

Duntulm Castle, guarded on three sides by sheer cliffs, dates from the Iron Age when it was first used as an Iron Age broch. History suggests that it became a Pictish fort before becoming the stronghold of the Vikings. James V of Scotland visited the castle in 1540 during his journey around the Highlands, attempting to bring an end to the feuding between local clans. The castle was eventually abandoned in 1730. Documentary evidence from 1880 suggests that the castle once stood several storeys high. Very little now remains of the original 17th-century structure, the disrepair augmented by a storm in 1980 that felled one of the last remaining masonry walls. Some of the castle stonework is reputed to have been used for local building in the past.

The castle is said to be haunted by several past inhabitants, including Hugh MacDonald who was imprisoned and left to starve to death in the dungeon for an attempt to take the land belonging to the MacLeods. Legend has it that he was driven mad and tried to eat his hands before dying. Another legend tells of a nursemaid who is said to wander through the ruined castle, having been killed for accidentally dropping the baby boy of the clan chief from a castle window onto the rocks below. She was holding him aloft for the chief returning from a voyage at sea. This tragic accident and subsequent haunting were cited as the reason for the abandonment of the castle.

The view to Tulm Island.

Tulm Bay, Duntulm Castle and the west coast of Trotternish.

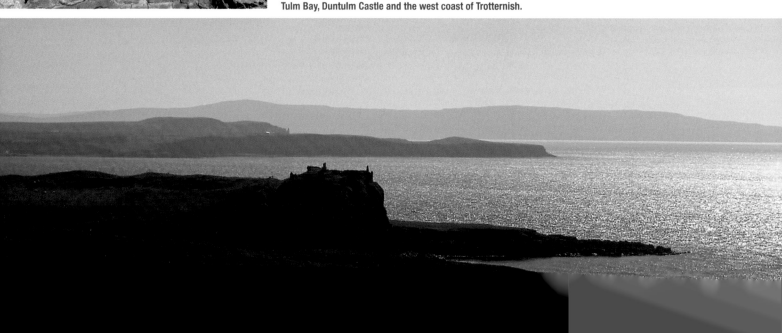

Return to the single-track road, turning left to initially gain height. Once the road begins to descend, the former coastguard cottages come into view with a small loch beyond. Before reaching the cottages at a bend in the road, take the track next to the hotel down to the sea. The hotel provides a delightful spot to rest a while for refreshment before the main part of the walk begins, particularly if the weather is in good form, with the panorama of Tulm Bay and Duntulm Castle stretched out before you.

Continue down the track to the coast below the castle to follow the rocky shoreline heading in the direction of the distant headland of Meall Tuath. The grassy foreshore makes for easy walking, with the delightful rocky coastline frequently tempting you to the water's edge.

Thrift flowers freely on the rocky outcrops during the summer months. More commonly known as sea pink, it is abundant throughout Skye during late spring and early summer, producing a wonderful display of colour. In contrast to the beautiful displays of wild flowers, a fascinating variety of seaweed can be found, clinging to the rocks between high and low water. At the point where the shore meets the lower slopes of Meall Tuath you are forced inland gaining height by crossing a stile. The area is sometimes boggy but is covered with sporadic crops of cotton grass dancing in the gentlest of breezes during the summer months. The upper slopes are clad in heather and gorse until the highest ground is reached where walking is now on short turfs.

Thrift, more commonly known as sea pink, is abundant on coastal rocks throughout Skye during spring and early summer, producing a wonderful display of colour. Thrift can also be seen growing on the slopes of the higher mountainous regions of Skye, somehow growing from what appears just a small crack in the rock.

107

Seaweed, Tulm Bay.

Once the higher ground is attained, you are rewarded with magnificent views to the northern most point of Skye. Rubha Hunish is set out below like a giant map with the distant islands of Gearran, Gaeilavore and Fladda-chuain, where the remains of a chapel dedicated to St Columba can be found, rising from the waters of the Little Minch some three miles off shore. During November 2002 HMS *Trafalgar*, a 4,750 tonne nuclear submarine ran aground during a training exercise on the uninhabited craggy rocks off Fladda-chuain, with the damage estimated to have cost in the region of £5 million. On the horizon can be seen the Isle of Harris, some 16 miles distant.

The descent to Rubha Hunish from Meall Tuath is to be found almost concealed behind a large rocky outcrop at the edge of the towering cliffs. The route down is severe for the first part and may not be to the liking of all, so it might be as well to admire the outstretched promontory from above. The views from the basalt-columned cliffs are some of the best to be found in Britain.

Fascinating colours contrast on the shores below Duntulm Castle. The view north west across Tulm Bay to Tulm Island takes in the distant remote small isles of Gearran, Gaeilavore and Fladda-chuain.

Rubha Hunish from Meall Tuath the most northerly point on Skye. Three miles off shore lie the small islands of Gearran, Gaeilavore and Fladda-chuain. During November 2002 HMS *Trafalgar*, a 4,750 tonne nuclear submarine, ran aground during a training exercise off the craggy rocks of Fladda-chuain.

Soon the old coastguard hut comes into view, complimenting the landscape, its bright white walls reflecting the summer sun set against the azure background 300ft above the sea. The former coastguard building overlooking the Little Minch would have been initially manned around the clock. The coastguard hut has been fully restored after suffering severe damaged during the great storm of January 2005, now used by The Mountain Bothies Association. The association is a charity looking after almost 100 shelters in some of the more remote parts of the British Isles.

Perhaps the best views of the basalt-columned cliff face can be gained if you have resisted the descent to Rubha Hunish by continuing along the cliff top to the right of the old coastguard hut.

Wild Hyacinth in Scotland, although known as Bluebell in England. Throughout late spring to early summer carpets of blue can be seen on the moorland and coastal fringes throughout Skye. This example is seen clinging to the craggy grass cliff top some 300ft above Loch Hunish on Meall Tuath.

The restored coastguard hut complements the landscape with its bright white walls reflecting the summer sun, seen here set against the azure background 300ft above Rubha Hunish on Meall Tuath.

The ruined croft houses of Erisco to this day reveal the craftsmanship of the crofters, being well preserved at ground level.

The return part of the walk begins here if you can tear yourself away from the views. Maintain a southerly direction following the sheep tracks over heather-clad turfs always above but toward the deserted crofts of Erisco, keeping the sea and Tulm Island on your right. The path keeps to the hillside, crossing a stile where you can drop down to take a closer look at the abandoned township. The crofts of Erisco were unusual in that they were built along a straight line, similar to the crofts on the remote islands of the St Kilda archipelago, a group of islands some 41 miles west of the Outer Hebrides. The crofters must have found it very hard to leave when the area was cleared as they had good grazing and easy access to the sea. Climb back to the escarpment to continue south-eastward, heading all the while for the sheep pens.

Common Cottongrass is a member of the sedge family growing on wet moorland and in boggy pools, a distinctive feature of the landscape of Skye. The flower head is an inconspicuous brownish colour that develops during the early summer into balls of long cotton-like hairs.

The abandoned township of Erisco was unusual in being built along a straight line similar to the abandoned crofts on the remote islands of the St Kilda archipelago. The crofters must have found it very hard to leave when the area was cleared as they had good grazing and easy access to the sea.

Throughout Skye the remains of ruined crofts from the Highland Clearances are still a dominant feature; although succumbed to vegetation, most still remain solid.

The northern-most extent of the Trotternish Ridge, Sgurr Mor stands over 1,600ft above sea level and dominates the distant landscape looking south east from the track above Erisco. Continue following the sheep paths where posts indicate the way, keeping the sheep pens on your right. Go through the gate to turn right to join the road, passing the phone box. A short period of easy road walking will bring you to the delightful Loch Cleat and the former coastguard cottages at Duntulm. The single-track road continues upward past the hotel before descending back to the start of the walk.

The spectacular Trotternish Ridge is an inland cliff that runs for almost 20 miles, winding its way along the spine of the peninsula from Portree in the south to its northern extent.

The ridge is made up of several pinnacles and peaks set against a backdrop of steep cliff faces. The most notable of the pinnacles is the Old Man of Storr, appearing to be precariously balanced on the slopes of the Storr. The pinnacle is a spectacular sight that can be seen from many vantage points and stands over 160ft high, a fascinating sight that awaits as we head southward down the east coast of Trotternish.

Head for the sheep pens to return to the road, and pass the brightly painted phone box on the last leg of this most pleasing of walks.

A close inspection of the stone work reveals the skill of the crofter.

Corran, Staffin Bay, provides a spectacular view of the northern most end of the Trotternish Ridge and is home to remarkably well-preserved dinosaur prints, at times visible on an ebbing tide.

Staffin Bay

Leaving behind the most northerly part of Skye, we now return south to find Staffin Bay and the coastal settlement of Staffin, 'The Place of Pillars'. The name originates from the Vikings referring to the basalt columns of the cliffs. The Jurassic rocks of this coast have revealed a fascinating insight into the past, with an impressive array of dinosaur remains being discovered. At Corran, fossilised dinosaur footprints can be found at low tide, although at times they are buried beneath the sand.

It is believed that the leader of Staffin sent a message to John MacPherson of Milovaig during the period of unrest telling him to 'stretch the law but do not break it'. At Staffin a single-track road forks right, leading to the small settlements of Marishader and Garros. Marishader was the home to the Martins of Marishader, famous in Skye's history for Martin Martin author of *A Description of The Western Isles*.

Legend has it that the two stone pillars standing on the moor near to Garros mark the site where two foolish brothers were said to have fought to the death for an inheritance.

A mile out of Staffin we come across Loch Mealt and a most impressive waterfall close to Kilt Rock.

Information signs provide detail to the most significant parts of Trotternish.

Mealt Waterfall fed from Loch Mealt freefalls into the Sound of Raasay 170ft below.

The spectacular rock formation known at Kilt Rock takes its name from the massive columns of dolerite, giving the appearance of pleats in a tartan kilt. Although not identical, they are similar to the basalt rocks at Staffa near Iona that are said to have been formed over 55 million years ago. Mealt Waterfall at grid reference 508 655 has the splendid backdrop of Kilt Rock, fed by Loch Mealt, the water freefalling into the Sound of Raasay 170ft below.

Staffin takes its name from the Viking 'The Place of Pillars', named after the basaltic columned cliffs.

A glimpse of the ridge from the same location looking north.

Trotternish Ridge

The vast inland cliff was formed around 50 million years ago when over 20 layers of volcanic rock were laid down, and the sedimentary rocks which had been covered by the flows of basalt lava eventually collapsed under the weight. The result of this huge landslip, the largest in the British Isles, was the creation of the most spectacular, surreal landscape we see today.

Most of the ridge is easily accessible, with the majority of the walking on turf paths. The whole route can be walked in two days, but the area can be treacherous, with mists seemingly descending from nowhere that have been known to last for several days.

The ridge looking south. Standing forward of the ridge is Cleat at 860ft, with Druim an Ruma over 1,000ft and the main ridge at 1,400ft providing the back drop. Further south is Beinn Edra, a little less than 2,000ft. The ridge is fairly straight forward, walking on grassy sometimes boggy ground, and can be walked in two days. Mists can descend onto the summits seemingly from nowhere and have been known to linger for several days on the highest peaks.

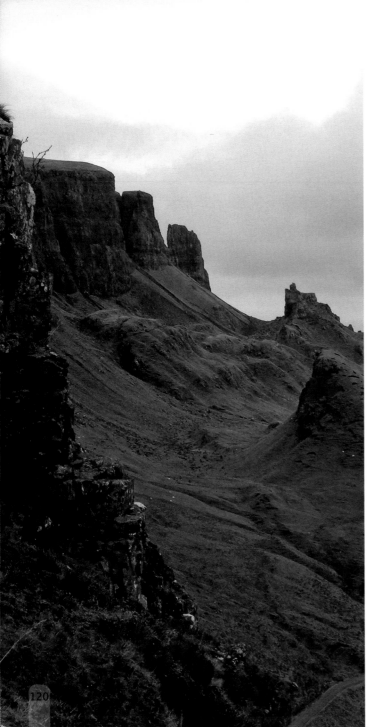

Looking north toward the Quiraing. The imposing cliffs of Meall na Suiramach, with the ridge height of over 1,700ft and opposite the massive rock known as The Prison, with an almost sheer face on one side and very steep grassy slopes on the other.

The ridge is traversed by a single-track road linking Staffin with the main port to the western isles, Uig. To the north of the single-track road is the Quiraing with the imposing cliffs of Meall na Suiramach over 1,700ft above sea level. Opposite the tall cliff is a massive rock known as The Prison, an almost sheer face on one side and very steep grassy slopes on the other. The Needle, The Table and several other striking features bedeck the area, the ridge providing breathtaking views over Staffin Bay and across the sea to Wester Ross.

The most famous landmark on Skye has to be the Old Man of Storr, the final goal in our journey of discovery, perhaps the most mysterious and eerie destination on Skye, perched below the tallest part of the ridge. The Storr has featured in many TV and film productions, among these the 1975 film *The Land That Time Forgot* and the television series *Hamish Macbeth*.

The ridge from the highest point of the single-track road that links Staffin to Uig the main port. The route crosses the ridge at grid reference 439 679 at a height of 840ft with a particularly steep section close to the summit.

Beyond Loch Fada, the Cuillin Hills seem remarkably close with the low winter sun creating an eerie atmosphere. The main ridge of the Black Cuillin, consisting of 11 Munros, is obscured by the low cloud, number 12 being Bla Bheinn (Blaven) separated by Glen Sligachan. The summits of the lower Red Cuillin stand clear.

THE OLD MAN OF STORR WALK

A colossal pillar undercut at the base standing over 160ft-high set below the towering Storr, an inland cliff 2,360ft above sea level, the Old Man is by far the most famous of the pinnacles and peaks that abound in this area of Trotternish. The Old Man was first climbed in 1955 by the late Don Whillans, being graded a very severe climb.

The steep but easily navigable route leads you into the sanctuary (Coire Faoin), flanked by the pinnacles and pillars set beneath the ridges highest point. When mists descend and melt away from the summits in a short space of time it creates a constantly changing eerie atmosphere that adds to this mysterious place.

Distance 3 miles, with an estimated time of 3–3.5 hours.

Park in the lay-by at grid reference 508 528 on the Portree to Staffin road. Go through the gate where detailed information about the Storr can be found, then follow a clearly defined path up through the forest. The first part of the climb is quite steep in places with no extended views, although the path having been rebuilt by the Skye and Lochalsh Footpath Trust makes for relatively steady progress. As you continue to climb higher, look for breaks in the trees providing tantalising views across the Sound of Raasay, and onward to the mountains of Applecross on the mainland.

As you leave the forest behind pass through a gate and look up in awe at the massive inland cliffs of the Storr. Depending on the light, you may need to look a second time to pick out the Old Man and the other pinnacles as they can merge into the background. A few seconds of concentration, though, and they will soon become foremost features in the midst of this surreal landscape.

Emerging from the conifer plantation, the full extent of the sheer cliff face of the Storr with the Old Man below is revealed, creating an awe-inspiring mysterious landscape. Mists can often envelope the summits, adding to the surreal atmosphere.

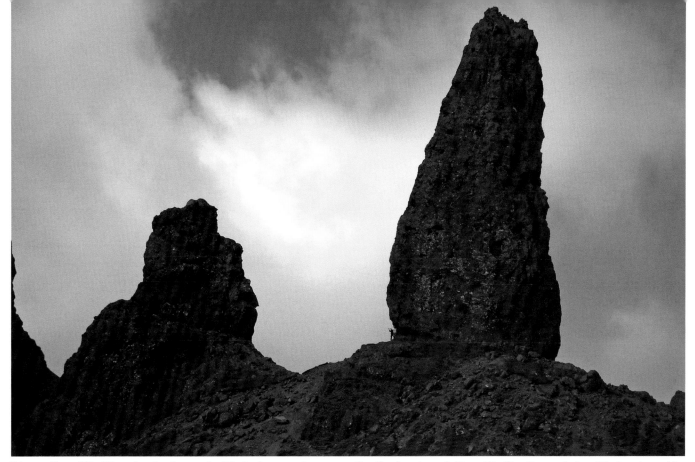

It is sometimes difficult to portray the sheer scale of the landscape, and no more so than the pinnacles and pillars of the Storr. You may just spot the two chaps at the base of the Old Man, giving some perception to the true size of this magnificent giant.

The path climbs ever higher and closer to the strange pinnacles and peaks, with a variety of tracks available to reach our goal. With the view now spread out behind you, a section of well-laid stone path branches off to your left, at first taking you away from the Old Man as it climbs steeply, soon it circles its way back in the right direction. Stop for a while and marvel at the view behind you to Loch Leathan and Loch Fada, their waters supplying the small hydro-electric power station below the cliffs on the shore at Bearreraig Bay.

The path snakes its way around the contours ever upward until you reach the foot of the Old Man. You are now in a surreal world, with the sanctuary set below and above the dark, craggy, unstable cliff face of the Storr, while to the north of the Old Man stands Needle Rock. The best way to photograph the Old Man getting a true perspective of its size has to be with fellow walkers standing at its undercut base. The Old Man can be circumnavigated, but only if you are reasonably confident to do so and should never be attempted in bad weather as mists will belie the hidden dangers.

The Old Man of Storr along with Needle Rock and the other pinnacles and pillars were formed when the sedimentary rocks which had been covered by basalt lava collapsed under the weight, thus forming the most spectacular landslip formations to be found anywhere in the British Isles. The mists create a surreal eerie atmosphere; even on a warm summer's day, the vortex of air sends a shiver down your spine.

The Sanctuary (Coire Faoin) flanked by the pinnacles and pillars set beneath the Storr, the ridge's highest point. When mists descend and disappear from the summits and pinnacles in a short space of time it creates a constantly changing atmosphere that adds to this mysterious place.

Some records note the height at 165ft, others a mere 160ft, but there is no doubt to the magnificence of the Old Man, a giant pinnacle that has withstood well the ravages of weather and time to remain a dominant feature of Trotternish. This was taken on a bright sunny day as mists suddenly shrouded the summit of the Storr, engulfing the Old Man and creating an incredible eerie atmosphere.

Coire Faoin, the sanctuary should not be missed. Follow the sheep tracks down to take in the tranquil atmosphere only broken occasionally by the distinctive call of ravens circling overhead. The view back to the Old Man perhaps may enlighten you as to the origin of its name. One theory goes that he lost his head in a storm in the late 1800s, while others differ, but I will leave that to your imagination.

How long you remain here before setting back on the return only time will tell, but what is certain are the pinnacles and pillars create a unique landscape of beauty and mystery.

The descent can be taken using one of several paths that lead you to the gate ahead of re-entering the forest. The views on the return part of this walk are on par with any we have been privileged to witness throughout Skye, Raasay extended before you from a shimmering sea and on the horizon the mountains of Wester Ross. The Cuillin, some 20 miles to the south, and the distant shores of Lochalsh can also be seen on a clear day.

The going is easier as you begin the descent into the wood, watching for rabbits that seem to forage without a care in the world as you pass by. The dense canopy of the conifer plantation is slowly being replaced with a return to planting of more native species. Continue downhill through the forest back to the car park.

Needle Rock, one of the impressive pinnacles of the Storr.

Alas, we have now reached the end of our journey discovering Skye. To those who are privileged to know this beautiful island intimately, there are many places we have not visited; indeed, there is nowhere on this enchanting island that is not deserving of a visit. What I have tried to achieve on the journey is to provide an insight for the visitor, and in particular the first-time visitor, to make possible an extensive array of coastal, mountain and historical sites that could be visited in a week. I would, though, recommend anyone planning to visit this beautiful island to stay a wee while longer. The walks featured range from a very easy stroll taking in the Coral Beaches to the more strenuous route to Camasunary, but like most things the reward is well worth the effort, particularly when Camasunary comes into view for the first time. The diversity of Skye's weather with all its changing moods and crystal-clear light generates a paradise for photographers. Yes, it does rain and the wind blows strong at times, but as the saying goes on Skye wait a short while and the sun will shine again. The weather is an important constituent to the dramatic scenes that unfold before you.

I have included brief notes on the islands sometimes turbulent past. Although it is not a thoroughly detailed history, I hope it has helped to provide you with an emotion of what makes this island so special.

I trust you have enjoyed the journey and it will inspire you to visit this wonderful island. You are assured of a warm welcome at any time of year. During the summer, Skye is blessed with long hours of daylight, so why not come 'over the sea to Skye' in the traditional way, by ferry from Glenelg. Come to the island in winter where both the wild stormy days and tranquil frosty ones will inspire you, the winter sun to be found low in the sky, creating perfect light for the photographer.